Praise for *An Unexpecte*

Struggling with questions of God's goodness and His love for you̲   ⸱
This book from Erica Wiggenhorn is for you! *An Unexpected Revival* will remind you that when all seems lost, God is always there, always working, always has your formation in mind. It will renew hope in your soul as you are reminded that He is the God who turns lifeless bones into armies of conquerors. You will be renewed with hope, strengthened, encouraged for the journey ahead as you walk with Jesus!

STEVE ENGRAM
Executive Director Venture Church Network and Lead Pastor of Desert Springs Community Church, Goodyear, AZ

I wish I could sit across from you in a café, sipping something rich and hot, something swirling with spices. I would look deep into your eyes and tell you about Erica's latest masterpiece, *An Unexpected Revival*. Its powerful flavors will jolt us awake to what God is up to in our world today. Our generation has entered a new season, and Erica challenges us—lovingly but firmly—to step into it as God's daughters and warriors, clothed for revival. Erica unveils that word, "revival," by diving deep into the mysterious book of Ezekiel. It is challenging and convicting. It is beautiful and eternal. Ezekiel's words are uncannily relevant today because our world is so eerily reminiscent of that wise old prophet's. So, drink deep, under Erica's sound guidance. *An Unexpected Revival* will taste of rainbow peppercorn and turmeric: daring, ambitious, maybe even overpowering at times, but most assuredly healing. I can't promise it will be easy, because truth cannot be sugarcoated. But I promise it will be good, because God is. Good for your soul, good for your relationship with Him, and good for those around you.

STEPHANIE ROUSSELLE
Founder and host of the top-ranking global podcast and eponymous ministries, GospelSpice

Erica Wiggenhorn does a masterful job of walking us through the book of Ezekiel in her newest Bible study, *An Unexpected Revival*. I've avoided studying Ezekiel because it seemed so difficult to understand—until now. Erica paints a picture for us in each chapter of what was happening at the time. She guides us through discovering the meaning and how we can make application to our lives today. This study on revival is very timely for the days we're living in. It makes me long for revival—in my heart, in my country, in the world.

CRICKETT KEETH
Women's Ministry Director; author of *On Bended Knee* and *Before the Throne*

If ever there was a time in history when we needed revival, it's now! Erica invites us into the wild and wonderful prophecies of Ezekiel. If your spirit is weary and your bones feel dry, this is your study! Dive into Ezekiel for *An Unexpected Revival*, and your soul will be refreshed!

BECKY HARLING
Conference speaker, coach, and author of *The Extraordinary Power of Praise*

Author Erica Wiggenhorn has done it again with her newest Bible study on Ezekiel, *An Unexpected Revival*. She's taken us deep into God's Word, sharing insight and application that will strengthen your walk with the Lord. Her foundation of biblical knowledge, coupled with her humble transparency, makes this a must-read for all believers.

EDIE MELSON
Director of the Blue Ridge Mountains Christian Writers Conference and award-winning author

Many years ago, during a season when I was desperately searching for God, I was invited to walk through the pages of Ezekiel with a few fellow military spouses. With Erica Wiggenhorn as our guide, we experienced unexplainable transformation—transformation that prepared our hearts with a spark of revival. With God's Word in hand, we found ourselves deeper and deeper in love with the person and work of Jesus. We discovered God in new and fresh ways. Ultimately, we found our God invites us to be closer to Him—with our doubts, despair, and dread in tow. In *An Unexpected Revival*, you will explore the prophecies of Ezekiel and ponder them with the voice of a trusted friend. Erica's heart for ardent Bible study, complete exposition, and Spirit-filled teaching lights the way to hearing what God has to say about Himself and what He is like. I hope you will accept this invitation to move beyond your doubt to a place of devotion.

MEGAN B. BROWN
Author of *Summoned: Answering a Call to the Impossible*

I started this study thinking, "Oh my goodness, how will I ever get through the book of Ezekiel?!" But after the first week, I couldn't put it down. Erica Wiggenhorn has taken the strange visions and prophecies of Ezekiel and made them approachable and applicable. This study will encourage you and embolden you. A revival *is* possible. Dive into this study and feel the Word of God stir you up and make you want more from your Christian life!

KIM ERICKSON
Author of *Surviving Sorrow: A Mother's Guide to Living with Loss* and *His Last Words: What Jesus Taught and Prayed in His Final Hours*

An Unexpected Revival is a timely Bible study for our generation that reminds us that genuine revival doesn't always look like what we think it might. Misconceptions of how God orchestrates revival are shattered as Erica takes us on a journey to grasp the message of the book of Ezekiel. This study will bring you to a fresh depth of understanding of the pathway to revival. If you long for more of Jesus, then *An Unexpected Revival* is a Bible study that will challenge your thinking and reshape your soul.

CYNTHIA CAVANAUGH
Author of *The Godly Kings of Judah: Faithful Living for Lasting Influence*

An Unexpected Revival is a study that will spark a fire in your heart that will turn you into a bold Christ follower with a passion for giving your all to Jesus. It will transform your life by igniting your spirit with fresh faith, renewed hope, and a reawakened purpose. Erica Wiggenhorn's challenge to immerse yourself in God's faithfulness, even in the middle of uncertainty, strikes a chord in my heart. Ask a group of friends to join you in this study. It shook me to my core.

CAROL KENT
Speaker and author, *He Holds My Hand: Experiencing God's Presence and Protection*

We are ALL in need of *An Unexpected Revival*! With wisdom and clarity, Erica guides the reader through the book of Ezekiel with personal, powerful, and peace-giving moments with God.

PAM FARREL
Author of fifty-six books, including bestselling *Discovering Hope in the Psalms: A Creative Bible Study Experience*

AN
8-WEEK
BIBLE
STUDY
OF
EZEKIEL

An
UNEXPECTED
REVIVAL

EXPERIENCING
GOD'S GOODNESS
through
DISAPPOINTMENT
and DOUBT

ERICA WIGGENHORN

MOODY PUBLISHERS
CHICAGO

© 2022 by
ERICA WIGGENHORN

Some portions of this book are adapted from Erica Wiggenhorn, *Ezekiel: Every Life Positioned for Purpose: Knowing Our God and Understanding Our Calling* (2011).

Scripture quotations are taken from the *ESV® Bible (The Holy Bible, English Standard Version®)*, Copyright © 2001 by Crossway, a publishing ministry of Good News Publishers. Used by permission. All rights reserved.

Published in association with The Steve Laube Agency, 24 W. Camelback Rd., A-635, Phoenix, AZ 85013.

Emphasis to Scripture has been added by the author.

Edited by Pamela Joy Pugh
Interior design: Kaylee Dunn
Cover design: Erik M. Peterson
Cover illustration of wave pattern copyright © 2020 by sunwart / Shutterstock (1849500643). All rights reserved.
Author photo: Sarah Hoag Photography

Library of Congress Cataloging-in-Publication Data

Names: Wiggenhorn, Erica, author.
Title: An unexpected revival : experiencing God's goodness through disappointment and doubt- an 8-week Bible study on Ezekiel / Erica Wiggenhorn.
Description: Chicago : Moody Publishers, 2022. | Includes bibliographical references. | Summary: "An engaging study of Ezekiel, An Unexpected Revival is an eight-week Bible study comprising five lessons per week. Author and speaker Erica Wiggenhorn examines God's call to Ezekiel, a major yet lesser-known biblical figure, who speaks to his fellow exiles in Babylon during a sobering but fascinating period in Israel's history. God's people are called to turn back from wrong ways and return to the God who's calling for a restored relationship with Him: in short, revival. "Revival is not a discovery of new information. Revival is a miraculous work of transformation as the Holy Spirit remolds and remakes our hearts and captivates our minds by His power," says the author"-- Provided by publisher.
Identifiers: LCCN 2021058362 (print) | LCCN 2021058363 (ebook) | ISBN 9780802425003 (paperback) | ISBN 9780802475428 (ebook)
Subjects: LCSH: Bible. Ezekiel--Textbooks. | BISAC: RELIGION / Biblical Studies / Bible Study Guides | RELIGION / Christian Living / Spiritual Growth
Classification: LCC BS1545.55 .W54 2022 (print) | LCC BS1545.55 (ebook) | DDC 224/.406--dc23/eng/20220125
LC record available at https://lccn.loc.gov/2021058362
LC ebook record available at https://lccn.loc.gov/2021058363

Originally delivered by fleets of horse-drawn wagons, the affordable paperbacks from D. L. Moody's publishing house resourced the church and served everyday people. Now, after more than 125 years of publishing and ministry, Moody Publishers' mission remains the same—even if our delivery systems have changed a bit. For more information on other books (and resources) created from a biblical perspective, go to www.moodypublishers.com or write to:

Moody Publishers
820 N. LaSalle Boulevard
Chicago, IL 60610

1 3 5 7 9 10 8 6 4 2

Printed in the United States of America

To Tami-

I'll never forget that day in the cafe when you shared with me the story of the two sisters in Scotland who faithfully prayed in their cottage sparking the Hebrides revival. With a gleam in your eye and a grin on your face you pounded the table and said, "Sister, let's lock arms and ask God to do it again!". Our weekly prayers are truly one of God's greatest gifts in my life. I love you, sister!

CONTENTS

The world can no longer be left to mere diplomats, politicians, and business leaders. They have done the best they could, no doubt. But this is an age for spiritual heroes— a time for men and women to be heroic in their faith and in spiritual character and power. The greatest danger to the Christian church today is that of pitching its message too low.

—Dallas Willard, *The Spirit of the Disciplines*

Inviting Revival

The number forty holds great significance throughout the Scriptures. The rain poured forty days over the ark while Noah and his family remained safe from the flood. Moses stayed away from Egypt for forty years while God prepared him to become the deliverer of Israel. Jesus faced temptation in the wilderness for forty days in preparation for His ministry. There are many other examples where we encounter the number forty and they encompass similar themes: purification, preparation, or fulfillment. My hope is that we see all three in our lives over the next forty days of this study.

May the Holy Spirit *purify* His church.
May the bride *prepare* for the return of her Bridegroom, making herself ready to do His work and His will.
May the work of the Holy Spirit be brought to *fulfillment* in the lives of all believers.

Doesn't that sound a whole lot like revival?

We need to start by shedding our misconceptions or expectations about how revival needs to look. Ezekiel certainly did. He thought revival would happen in Jerusalem, the religious epicenter of his nation. He thought God's glory would emanate from the temple. He thought it looked like political freedom, economic prosperity, and religious fervor. *And he was wrong.*

When you think of revival, what pictures come to your mind? Giant crowds? Megachurches? Emotional pleas from polished preachers? Certainly lots of church folk involved, right? We'd hope so.

The prophecies of Ezekiel give us a different picture of revival. The people God chose to spark revival were counted out, cast aside, displaced, and disregarded. They were the lot whom everyone decided God had forgotten. The ones out of favor, lacking supposed fervor, and forced into captivity by their enemies. In the Jewish way of thinking, removal from the land signified God's displeasure and a consequence for unfaithfulness. (See Deuteronomy 28:36–44.) People who believed their doubts and doubted their beliefs. But God insists those are the exact people ripe for revival. Seems so backwards, doesn't it?

I first started studying the book of Ezekiel over ten years ago. While making my way through the book, Don, one of our pastors, shared in a sermon about his time in Russia when the nation was under Communist rule.

He reminded us that any form of religious gathering or instruction remained strictly forbidden. Don told how he and another American pastor entered the country as businessmen while they smuggled in Bibles for the underground church.

Somehow this underground church in Moscow discovered that Don was a pastor. None of their church leaders in Russia had any sort of formal seminary training and they begged him to teach Scripture to them. He knew if he were to get caught he would immediately be imprisoned, leaving his wife stranded in Moscow, perhaps also to be arrested. As the faces of his family members flashed through his mind, he sensed the Holy Spirit leading him to stay and teach through the night. He knew it could be a year or more before another pastor able to teach the Bible came to their city. For the next six hours he walked these fervent Russian believers through the book of Romans, explaining God's plan to bring all people to repentance, the work of the Holy Spirit in their lives, and even why God allows suffering. Don assured them of the immutable grace of God and their unalterable security in His love. Hundreds of Russians huddled together hanging on every word. Believers were encouraged and revived. Dozens gave their lives to Christ that night for the first time.

At the end of the six hours, Don closed with Paul's great prayer in Romans 15:13 over the ancient Roman church that had stood persecuted by the Roman Empire: "May the God of hope fill you with all joy and peace in believing, so that by the power of the Holy Spirit you may abound in hope."

As he told that story to our church, he concluded, "There's no greater thing in this life than serving Jesus. There's nothing worth risking your life for more than the gospel of Christ. I found out a year later that this church in Moscow had tripled in size in just a few short months."

As he told that story something bubbled up inside of me. I wanted to teach the Scriptures to those who had no one else to bring God's Word to them. Those who were starving to be fed the life-giving nourishment of the Word and consumed it with great delight. I wanted to see revival.

As I drove home from church that day, I took the usual route, driving past the women's prison. I had passed it hundreds of times before, never giving it a second thought. As I waited at a stoplight, the Holy Spirit nudged my heart. "Right there, go take My Word to the women inside." Since I don't have a lot of those clear-cut moments with God, I doubted I had heard His voice and chalked up the words to my imagination.

Two days later I walked into the Tuesday morning Bible study at church and found a new woman sitting at my table. I introduced myself and welcomed her. She informed me that she had been asked to visit and share about her ministry. Our pastor's wife invited her onto the stage and she began to share. She ran a prison ministry and they needed volunteers. I felt the nudge again, sensing God's message. "Ezekiel and his captives were those I imprisoned in order to set them spiritually free. I came to set the captives free and I am asking you to go teach them My Word." I knew God was calling me to this, so I (rather cowardly) approached the woman afterward. Three months later I was inside the prison mentoring a young woman, and six months later I was leading a Bible study there.

I love Jesus' promise in John 8:36—"So if the Son sets you free, you will be free indeed."

So it was with the women in the prison who had met Jesus. They remained behind bars but were set free spiritually. They found a peace and a security they had never known, and their current captivity mattered little to them in comparison to the freedom they had found in Christ Jesus. They experienced revival. They had lived in the dark and now basked in the warm glow of the light of Christ. They were the walking dead who had found everlasting life. I realized now what Paul meant when he wrote, "Awake, O sleeper . . . and Christ will shine on you" (Eph. 5:14). While I believed in Jesus, I still lived in the shadows of my faith. I wanted the joy and peace these women had. I wanted revival. And I found it in the most unexpected of places: our state prison yard. *Just like Ezekiel.*

How about you? How desperately do you want revival? Would you go anywhere to witness it? Would you risk your freedom or even your life for it as Pastor Don did? Is your heart open and looking for it even in the unexpected places? Abraham found it in a desolate desert. Moses found it on the edge of civilization in a burning bush. Elijah found it in a snarky, unbelieving pagan woman's home. John the Baptist found it in the blazing Judean desert. Peter found it in an empty fishing net he could not find a way to fill. Paul found it on a murderous mission. John Mark found it through the shame of quitting and disappointing his leaders. All pretty unexpected places, wouldn't you agree?

Will you open your heart to revival these next forty days? Will you allow God to reveal to you any area of your heart or life in which He longs to work but you remain closed to Him? Will you invite God to prepare, purify, and fulfill His work in you that you might shine the light of Christ in our generation? Jesus chose a woman, Mary Magdalene, to be the first to witness His resurrection. May He choose every woman who opens the pages of this study to experience His revival.

REVVING UP REVIVAL IN YOUR STUDY TIME

My assumption, dear one, is that revival is something dear to your heart in choosing to complete this study, or you are curious as to what revival truly is. You long to grow closer to God, deeper in your understanding of His Word and higher in your faith in its promises and His power. I long for those things for you as well, and for me. But most importantly, God does.

We must start by making one point abundantly clear. **Revival is not a discovery of new information. Revival is a miraculous work of transformation as the Holy Spirit remolds and remakes our hearts and captivates our minds by His power.** Paul told the Ephesian believers that the same power that rose Jesus from the dead resides within us. That power is a person: the Holy Spirit. He is the power behind revival. He illuminates the Word of God, He renews our mind, and He heals our heart. We cannot experience revival without Him. Which means, going through a workbook will prove useless without His work within us. So we must begin every lesson with prayer.

Let's pray together now: *Holy Spirit, renew my mind, convict my heart, heal my heart, and empty me of myself, making more room for You.*

Second, we must look at these daily lessons as appointments, not assignments, as scheduled time with God to do His work within us. Don't rush through them. Don't try to cram them all into completion before you head into your class or group study. Sit and savor the beauty of the Savior and the majesty of God. Read the passage at the beginning of each day aloud, taking it all in with multiple senses. Then begin to work through the lesson after you have given your full attention to the Word itself. These appointments with God grow your intimacy with Him, building your trust in both His character and His capabilities. Take time to invest in your relationship with Him. Revival is an experience—it involves your mind and your emotions, which cannot happen outside of relationship.

Third, do what you can. Life gets busy. Things happen. Don't beat yourself up when you get off track or fall behind. Do what you can do and commit to attending weekly to meet in community to finish the study. If you are planning to do this study alone, prayerfully consider who you might ask to join you. We learn better together. And I am always here for you if I can answer any questions or pray for you along the way. Feel free to contact me at support@ericawiggenhorn.com.

Finally, take advantage of the supplemental resources available to you to enhance your study time. To access the supplemental teaching videos that accompany this study, visit www.vimeo.com and type "An Unexpected Revival" into the search bar. You can also go to ericawiggenhorn.com/books to access the free leader's and listening guides, and you can even download my free eBook *Praying Revival Prayers* there. These sample prayers include praying revival for your marriage, family, children, church, community, and our nation.

I am praying for you, dear one. I believe God is ready and willing to do a fresh work in us if we will seek His face and ask Him for it. Did you hear that? I think I hear a fresh wind beginning to stir . . .

A BRIEF HISTORICAL SYNOPSIS

The prophecies of Ezekiel prove difficult and most of us have probably been taught little from these strange visions and prophecies. Before we begin, a brief understanding of the history of Israel helps us put Ezekiel's messages in context. This portion of Israel's history proves most significant because it points to a deeper need for their Messiah beyond a desire to be an independent nation. The role and work of Messiah involved spiritual restoration between God and His people. He would bring revival.

Back in 2 Samuel 7:1–17, God had promised King David that one of his descendants would remain on the throne in perpetuity. After the death of David's son, King Solomon, in 931 BC, Israel split into two nations—the northern section, Israel, and the southern section, Judah. Israel comprised ten of the twelve tribes of the original nation, while Judah was made up of the remaining two tribes: Benjamin and Judah. David, who was from the tribe of Judah, continued to have a descendant sit on the throne in Jerusalem. God's promise stood. In 722 BC, the northern portion, Israel, fell to the Assyrian Empire. Judah remained a nation, along with God's promise to have a descendant of David on the throne in Jerusalem.

At the opening of the scene of Ezekiel, Nebuchadnezzar has attacked Judah and removed their king, Jehoiakim, bringing him to Babylon. His son Jehoiachin becomes king of Judah for just a few months until he himself is taken to Babylon along with thousands of other captives. The promise still remains thus far, however, because rather than instituting a foreign ruler, Nebuchadnezzar placed Zedekiah, Jehoiakim's uncle, on the throne of Judah as vassal. So one of David's descendants continues to reign in the city of Jerusalem, albeit as a puppet king under the rule of the king of Babylon. The prophecies of Ezekiel proved unfathomable to the exiles primarily because he spoke of a seeming break in the promise of God to David: "Your throne shall be established forever" (2 Sam. 7:16). How could the temple and the city of Jerusalem be entirely destroyed without this promise being broken?

Those who remained within the walls of Jerusalem asserted that punishment had already been issued on the exiles. The city now purged, they remained safely inside its walls. God however, speaks to the exiles in a strange twist of plans. He would shelter the exiles in a foreign land and destroy those who remained within the city walls. He would reestablish David's throne as promised in Ezekiel 36–37 and would rebuild their temple.

Thus, the messianic component of Ezekiel's prophecies. For David's throne to remain in perpetuity, it must constitute a greater throne than David's.

An unshakable kingdom. Messiah's kingdom. Ezekiel awakens the reader to understand Messiah's kingdom to be something more than merely a physical kingdom, but also a spiritual one. In this kingdom, God Himself, through Messiah, yet again rules and reigns in the midst of His people, just as He originally intended back in Exodus 25:8: "And let them make me a sanctuary, that I may dwell in their midst."

As hearers of Ezekiel's prophecies today, we must ask ourselves, Do we merely desire a physical church, with traditions and tangible practices, or do we desire to abide with God and receive a new heart and a newly revived life?

A STARTLING REVIVAL

When Circumstances Don't Match Our Expectations

GONE BUT NOT FORGOTTEN

EZEKIEL 1

Have you ever had a morning when you glanced at the clock, saw it was well before noon, and you felt like you had already run a marathon? I personally have never run a marathon, but if the exhaustion I felt after hobbling my way through a 5K is any indication of what it might feel like, well then, no thank you! I'll leave the marathon running to those more disciplined and courageous than I am!

But we've all had those mornings, haven't we? The trip to work was exceedingly hectic and you felt behind before you even arrived. The morning routine to get the kids to or through the school day felt like two steps forward and ten steps back. You were up all night with crying little ones you could not console. You wrestled in prayer for your spouse or loved one who was weathering a difficult season. You needed to reprimand your difficult coworker—again. You wondered how you might rekindle life in an empty nest or home upon the departure of those you love most dearly.

Life. Sometimes it's a hard journey. Some of us may feel like we're running in a marathon right now. On those days, when I feel like I'm chugging and puffing and barely making headway, I get discouraged. I begin to ask myself questions: "What am I here for?" and "Is this really the way life is supposed to be?" Sometimes I ask the more poignant question: "What is my purpose, anyway?" I grasp this idea in my head that if I am truly walking with the Lord, then life shouldn't feel like such a marathon. It should feel more like a walk in the park—peaceful and enjoyable.

God led Ezekiel on a long and arduous journey, over seven hundred miles from the city of Jerusalem where he had lived all of his life, to a settlement for exiled prisoners in the nation of Babylon. Now, before you take off your running shoes and claim that you are not in the mood to read about somebody else's bad news, take another swig of cold water and keep reading. What Ezekiel reckoned to be the ruin of his life actually placed him on a path of revival. God restored His relationship with His people, recaptured their hearts in revival, and awakened them to great purpose through Ezekiel's faithful obedience.

The living, active, Word of God spells out for us in Ezekiel's vivid and powerful messages *who we are and what we are to be doing*. It places our ultimate purpose before us in flashing neon lights. Ezekiel's name means "God strengthens," which aptly reminds us that most stages of life require God's endurance to pursue the path of purpose He has for us. Can I get an amen? So, friend, I hope you'll lace up those running shoes, hiking boots, or slide securely into those flip flops—God longs to bring revival to us today as well and rebuild those places ravaged by loss, awakening us to the greatest purpose in history!

READ EZEKIEL 1:1–9.

What is the date that Ezekiel records?

Where is Ezekiel living and with whom?

What did Ezekiel see and from which direction did it arrive?

Ezekiel's father was a priest. At Ezekiel's current age of thirty, he would have begun serving in the temple in Jerusalem as a priest as well. Instead he sits exiled in Babylon. Ezekiel is in a place of despondency. He is a prisoner taken far away from home with his purpose in life stripped from him. He would have spent nearly all of his life preparing for the priesthood and now such service was impossible, as he and his fellow exiles were far away from the temple in Jerusalem with little to no hope of immediate return. He informs us that he has already been in Babylon for five years and with each passing day, hope waned.

Have you ever had a dream or a goal for your life for which you spent years of your time and energy preparing? If so, what was it?

Did the Lord have you persist on that path for your life, or did He point you in another direction? How did the change or the fulfillment of your dream or goal make you feel?

Ezekiel's call comes at a very difficult time in his life. He records the exact dates of the call, possibly to authenticate for his audience, the other exiles, that the vision received is truly from the Lord. He begins his vision with a "stormy wind came out of the north." Nebuchadnezzar, the king of Babylon, had invaded Israel from the north, but Ezekiel is not describing the arrival of an earthly king here; he's describing the arrival of one much greater.

Nebuchadnezzar, the king of Babylon, was rising as the next world power. The northern portion of Israel had already been defeated by the Assyrians over one hundred years prior. The southern portion of Israel, referred to historically as Judah, continued to have a king on the throne. Nebuchadnezzar had previously invaded Judah, but simultaneously fought the Egyptians, Assyrians, Tyrians, and many other Canaanite tribes. The exiles hoped they could soon return home and that the king of Babylon would focus further military exploits away from Judah, leaving their beloved temple in Jerusalem intact, securing God's promise to eternally keep a king on the throne in Jerusalem.

The Jews of Ezekiel's day believed that God dwelt in the temple of Jerusalem. Being exiled in Babylon meant that they were far removed from the presence of the Lord and had presumably lost His favor. (See Moses' warnings to Israel in Deuteronomy 29:24–28.) Yet, Ezekiel speaking about a thick cloud coming was to remind them that the Lord was with them even in the land of the Babylonians (Nah. 1:3). He had not forgotten them.

Have you ever had a time or a circumstance in your life when you felt like the Lord had forgotten you?

The Lord has opened up the throne room of heaven and allowed Ezekiel to peer into His holy dwelling. Ezekiel is trying to describe for us what he sees there. As I am writing this, I am sitting in my friend's home peering out onto a beautiful lake in mid-August in Michigan. The scene is so lushly green and tranquil that I can't help but wish that my husband could see it. Unfortunately, he is back in Arizona where it is brown, dry, and scorching hot. I will go home and try to describe for him every detail of my friend's stunning panoramic lake view outside her window. However, no matter how many details I insert, it will prove difficult to know if he will really be able to fully appreciate what I am describing and if the mental pictures he will form in his mind will be completely accurate. Even several snapshots on my phone cannot do the entirety of the scene justice.

Ezekiel is describing a scene so breathtakingly awesome and of such beauty and perfection, we can only hope that the pictures we are forming in our mind bring God the glory due His Name. Even more importantly, we want to understand what God is trying to tell Ezekiel, and subsequently us, by allowing us the marvelous opportunity to get a sneak peek into heaven!

READ EZEKIEL 1:10–28.

These four living creatures are seraphs or the seraphim. Listen to this description by Matthew Henry:

> The scattered perfections of the living creatures on earth meet in the angels of heaven. They have the understanding of a man, and such as far exceeds it; they also resemble man in tenderness and humanity. But a lion excels man in strength, and boldness, therefore the angels, who in this resemble them, put on the face of a lion. An ox excels man in diligence, and patience, in the work he has to do; therefore, the angels, employed in the service of God, and the church, put on the face of an ox. An eagle excels man in quickness and piercing sight, and in soaring high; and therefore, the angels, who seek things above, and see far into divine mysteries, put on the face of a flying eagle.[1]

The wheels could go anywhere the Spirit of God led them. They had eyes all around. There is nothing beyond the sight or scope of God. He could see and reach His people in exile. Their placement served as part of His divine plan. The rainbow recalled God's promise to remember His promises (Gen. 9:16). Just like God was reminding Ezekiel and the exiles with him that God remembered them, so also, be reminded that God has not forgotten you. Wherever you are today, whether with dashed or fulfilled dreams, in a place of freedom or imprisonment, experiencing despondency or hope, God sees you. And just like Ezekiel and his fellow exiles, He has positioned you with purpose. Your circumstance may seem hopeless or the opposite of how you imagined your life to be at this point, but will you, like Ezekiel, fall facedown and listen to the voice of your God speak to you? The Lord has something to tell us in these next few weeks; will you posture your heart to receive it?

Spend a few moments in stillness committing to listen to what the Lord desires to say to you. Ask Him to ready you to receive the message that He has prepared for you and for grace to follow Him in obedience. Ask Him for eyes to see and a heart to believe that it is often in our most difficult or disappointing circumstances that we are ready to behold His goodness and glory! We become ready for revival.

RECEIVING THE CALL

EZEKIEL 2

I don't like cliff-hangers! "Happily ever afters" are my preferred conclusions. Yesterday ended abruptly in the middle of Ezekiel's vision. God ushering a man into His throne room hardly constitutes a typical storyline in Scripture, so what is God's purpose in bringing Ezekiel there?

Ezekiel witnessed the full glory of Yahweh—can you even imagine it?

Before we dive back into this wild scene today (yes, we're still cliff-hanging!), let's do a little recap. Ezekiel's audience are his fellow exiles. While God will tell him to prophesy against Jerusalem, the Israelites who remained within the walls of that city most likely never heard any of Ezekiel's messages, albeit one sent by messenger, which we can read in Jeremiah 29–33. Inside Jerusalem, Jeremiah served as prophet. Ezekiel is over seven hundred miles away in Babylon with fellow Israelite prisoners who had been captured by King Nebuchadnezzar. Daniel is also an exile in Babylon, serving as a captive in Nebuchadnezzar's royal court. Ezekiel's messages inform his fellow captors of the judgment and subsequent restoration God will bring to the city of Jerusalem along with His plans for them as political prisoners.

Before we delve too deeply into Ezekiel's prophecies, we ought to clarify a few things. God will often command Ezekiel to "speak to my people Israel," but at this point in history, as we saw in the earlier synopsis, Israel does not actually exist, since they are a conquered nation. When King Solomon died, the nation was divided over which son would ascend to the throne, resulting in the nation of Israel's spliting into northern and southern sections, in effect, two kingdoms. The north retained the name Israel and the southern portion was referred to as Judah. In 722 BC, the Assyrians conquered the tribes in the north (Israel) while Judah still remained an independent nation. Now Judah had been overcome by the king of Babylon, and the exiles wondered when and how this king, who had ordered their captivity, would be defeated. God referring to His people as "Israel" proves significant, because from God's vantage point, the nation of Israel will certainly exist again, and His people will inhabit it. For God to refer to Ezekiel's exilic audience as "Israel" heralded God's intent to eventually return them to their land and restore Israel as a nation. This would have proved comforting to them and reminded them of God's faithfulness.

We also need to remember that Ezekiel is not speaking to the people who are still living in Judah and Jerusalem; he is only speaking to his fellow exiles in Babylon, who have been deported from Judah as political prisoners. They were not actually locked up in cells in the way we think of a modern-day prison. But they were removed from their homeland and forced to move to another country. It might be difficult for us today to understand what this would entail, but what we must understand is that for the Jew, this development meant more than mere relocation and leaving all that was familiar to them behind (as traumatic as that in itself was). Removal from Jerusalem meant their inability to offer sacrifices in the temple. This proved devastating, since sacrificial worship in the temple was their sole means of securing God's favor and being absolved of sins. Furthermore, Jewish religious laws held rigid guidelines regarding social interaction among Gentiles and regarding food consumption. For those who had lived within the confines of Jerusalem and its surrounding countryside their entire lives, being surrounded by pagan temples, people of foreign tongue, and religious customs far different from their Jewish heritage would have been shocking to them. To be removed from their prescribed way of worshiping equated to their feeling of being out of favor with God. The captivity indeed was disastrous for the Jews.

READ EZEKIEL 2:1–10.

What did God command Ezekiel to do?

What emotion might Ezekiel succumb to in fulfilling this call?

To what unpleasant creature did God compare His people Israel?

(The ESV in verse 6 says "you sit on" and the NIV [2] uses the words "you live among." Either way, it's not a compliment!)

What did God command Ezekiel to eat?

Ezekiel beheld the radiance, majesty, and glory of God, witnessing His mighty angels ready and willing to do His bidding. God prepared Ezekiel for this call by first showing him the utter awesomeness of Who He Is. Think about your own prayer life and how you imagine God. How do you most often envision Jesus?

Sitting on a rock with little children around Him.

Holding a lamb.

Hanging on the cross.

In His glorified state.

Another way?

What if we pictured Jesus in His glorified state as Ezekiel did? How would that change our prayers, our faith, our submission and obedience to Him, and our regard of His holiness? In order to fulfill the call God was placing on his life, Ezekiel needed to be reminded that he served a mighty and powerful God. As do we! When we de-escalate Christ, we elevate doubt and fear!

Isn't it interesting that Ezekiel is held captive by a wicked nation as an enemy Jew, but God knows that he will fear his own countrymen over the Babylonians? Sometimes when called to serve, we can fear our own brothers and sisters in the church more than the enemy all around us. You saw that God refers to Ezekiel's fellow Jews as scorpions. Since we live in Arizona, scorpions are a very familiar fear. We've experienced the unexpected sting of a scorpion more than once in our home, needing hours of recovery from the numbness and the ache. When I think of scorpions, several descriptors come to mind: silent, concealed, operate in the darkness, sting to kill and devour. That's a strange way to describe Ezekiel's fellow Israelites. A scorpion is a hard-to-see predator that emerges unexpectedly.

I would bet that some of us have been unknowingly attacked and stung by some "scorpions" from whom we least expected it. God informs Ezekiel ahead of time that these attacks will come, but He didn't give Ezekiel a pass to get out of his calling as a result. We might want to hang up our service hat because we have gotten stung somewhere in the church or by a brother or sister in Christ, but just like Ezekiel, we shouldn't be surprised when we suffer some unexpected stings. Has the memory of a previous ache caused you to shrink back in fear? Has numbness remained long afterward causing you to pull away from your brothers and sisters? Before we start diving more fully into Ezekiel's calling and subsequently our own, let's pause right here and invite God to bring some additional healing into that hurt.

Jot down any names or painful circumstances that come to mind, asking God to bring healing.

Just as we must believe God can bring healing to our hurt, so we must trust God to strengthen us to fulfill any call He places on us. (See especially Ezekiel 2:2, 4.) God raised Ezekiel up and gave him the words to speak. Scripture makes no mention of God choosing Ezekiel due to any particular gifts or abilities held by him. Maybe it was simply Ezekiel's willingness to obey. We must never attempt to serve our all-powerful God in our own feeble strength.

Think of your own life for a moment. Can you think of a time when God called you to serve in a manner that caused you to be fearful or you doubted your ability? Recall what happened and imagine how this story might encourage someone else.

Reread Ezekiel 2:1–8 and circle how many times God uses some form of the word "rebel."

I think God used the word "rebellious" because He knew it would evoke an emotional response from Ezekiel's audience. They suffered the consequences of Israelite king Jehoiakim rebelling against Nebuchadnezzar, king of Babylon. The futility of this revolt remained daily before their eyes. They had been stripped of their possessions, positions, families, and seemingly God's presence, as their king's rebellion resulted in their imprisonment.

I can't help but rejoice in the faithfulness of Yahweh. Despite their actions and reactions, He continued to pursue His people. Though the Israelites had rebelled against Him, He continued to speak, imploring them to listen.

Listening is a choice.

Will we choose to listen? We must posture ourselves to listen. Ezekiel fell on his face and then heard the Lord speak. He postured himself for revival.

READ EZEKIEL 2:8–10.

What did the Lord give Ezekiel?

What was written on it?

What was he to do with it?

Sometimes what the Lord gives us feels frightening, uncomfortable, or downright difficult. Surely Ezekiel would have much preferred messages of hope, love, and forgiveness to share with his people, but that wasn't what the Lord was asking of him.

Is the Lord asking something hard of you today? How does reflecting on God's faithfulness embolden and empower you?

Close today asking Jesus to expand your vision of Him—high and lifted up, seated in glory. Ask Him to posture your heart to listen to Him and grace to be obedient in whatever direction He places on your life. (Yes, I know this is similar to yesterday, but just like Ezekiel and the exiles, we'll need repeated reminders to become awakened to our great purpose!)

TOUGH TO SWALLOW

EZEKIEL 3:1–18

Mary Poppins quipped, "A spoonful of sugar helps the medicine go down," but Ezekiel needs to swallow words of lamentation, mourning, and woe! In other words, what God will command Ezekiel to share won't be well received. It reminds me of when I have to tell my kids something I know they won't want to hear. They tune me out and pretend they can't hear me. When I force them to look at me so I can ensure they are actually listening, their eyes get that glazed-over look, letting me know that all they are actually processing sounds like, "Blah, blah blah, Mom's barking orders again!" Rarely do they jump right up in instant obedience. It usually takes a few reminders and prodding, and some squashing of their excuses, before my teens rush to respond.

Think about Ezekiel's audience for a moment, the thousands of captives. Their king, Jehoiakim, foolishly rebelled against Babylon, resulting in their deportation (2 Kings 24:14–16). They probably have left family members behind in Israel with whom they have no way of communicating. They are in a place of desperation. Now along comes Ezekiel, and he is going to speak to them words of lamentation, mourning, and woe—probably not on their top one hundred list of things they want to hear right now, and I'm sure Ezekiel knows it.

READ EZEKIEL 3:1–11.

God repeats His instructions to Ezekiel twice.

What does He tell Ezekiel to do first?

And then second?

How is the taste of the scroll described?

According to God, who would not listen to the messages sent, and who would?

With what phrase was Ezekiel to begin the messages?

What would God do for Ezekiel to enable him to faithfully deliver God's messages? (You might want to read vv. 8–9 in a couple of different versions.)

Does anyone else find it a bit odd that words of lamentation, mourning, and woe would taste as sweet as honey? The goodness of God turns even difficulty into victory, ravaging into restoration, and sadness to joy. In God's grace, He promised this to Ezekiel in the sweetness of the taste.

Ezekiel ate the scroll. He didn't just take the scroll from the Lord's hands, unroll it before the people and proclaim, "Thus says the LORD God!" He opened his mouth and he ate it and then the Lord said, "Go!" I think this order of events is significant. First of all, once he ate, the message became part of him. He fully committed himself to it. He filled himself with God's Word and then he went and spoke to the people.

The application here is simple: we too must first eat and then go. We cannot speak words of truth in our homes, churches, workplaces, and communities if we haven't eaten them ourselves by committing to fill our stomachs with God's Word.

God warns Ezekiel that the people most likely will not listen to his warnings or instructions. Ezekiel must be thrilled. God called him to stand up in front of his kinsmen, deliver a difficult message, and depend on their rejection. God explains, "But the people of Israel are not willing to listen to you because they are not willing to listen to me." Do you have someone in your life whose attention you are struggling to gain? Maybe it's a spouse, a stubborn child, a difficult boss, coworker, or friend. You are trying to speak truth into a person's life, but they refuse to listen. When we speak God's Word into a person's life and they reject the message, we should not take it personally. God spells out for us who they are ultimately rejecting.

READ JESUS' WORDS IN JOHN 15:18 AND 17:14.

What reactions did He receive to His message?

When we put ourselves out there trying to speak truth and the response is hurtful, we can know that Jesus understands. If you have someone you are trying to reach with truth, pray for that person right now. Ask God for the grace to release that person over to His care and to guard your heart from hurtful emotions.

Contrarily, those who would likely heed God's warnings to repent proved to be the opposite of whom we might think. Not Israelites, but foreigners. God would call Ezekiel to issue warnings to the surrounding nations inviting them to repent, just like He did Israel.

Read Psalm 119:18 and write it below.

Even God's warnings prove wonderful when we begin to understand their protection over us! When God places someone in our lives with whom we feel compelled to speak truth, we need to follow these directives God issued to Ezekiel:

1. Fear them not.

2. Receive God's Word in your heart and hear with your ears.

3. Tell them, "Thus says the Lord God . . ."

And then we pray, pray, pray! Don't give up on that person you long to see come to repentance. Ask God to harden your forehead and strengthen your resolve. God hasn't given up on Israel. He is committed to sending messages even though He knows very few of them will initially listen. We must have the same diligence in sharing His message of hope with a rebellious world!

IN THE MIDDLE OF THE HARD

EZEKIEL 3:12–28

Discovering God's will does not always prove to be easy. Often we question what God's will is for our lives and how we know when we are in it. Well, in the case of Ezekiel, God left no room for doubt. He called Ezekiel with a miraculous vision and then gave him specific instructions for carrying out the call. Let's review what God told him before we move into new territory.

In Ezekiel 3:9–11, God laid out three very clear directions:

1. Fear not your fellow Israelites.

2. Receive God's Word in your heart and hear it with your ears.

3. Speak God's Word(s) to the people.

If you are in a place where you desperately desire God to reveal His will to you in a certain area, pray through these commands of God. Are you harboring fear? Do you have a heart attitude that says, "Lord, I want to serve You, but please don't ask me to do *that*," because you are afraid of what *that* might entail? God tells Ezekiel, do not "be dismayed at their looks." In other words, do not fear their response or rejection. Maybe we need to bring some specific fears to the Lord before He is ready to make known His call to us. For someone who has a PhD in people-pleasing, I succumb to that fear of man's rejection all too easily.

Second, God told Ezekiel to receive God's Word with his heart and listen carefully with his ears. The numbing effects of familiarity easily settle in and, while God is speaking plain as day to us through an all too familiar passage, we sit back expecting Him to unveil some divine mystery we hadn't seen before. Occasionally God desires that which is familiar to our eyes to prick our heart anew with fresh wonder. Other times we get so busy telling the Lord all that we want Him to do that we fail to listen. Could it be that the Lord is already speaking, stirring our heart and prompting a passion, but we refuse to slow down long enough to let the truth penetrate through all of our noise? In our entire reading of Ezekiel thus far, how many words has Ezekiel spoken? None! He has done nothing but listen!

Third, God told him, "Speak to them and say to them, 'Thus says the Lord GOD.'" That word "speak" insinuates going after to discourse with them. We might say, "Go find so and so and say . . ." God instructs Ezekiel to be intentional about delivering His messages, not sit back and wait for the people to come seek him out. If I'm honest, I often want God to lay out the plans and then I'll get going. I don't want to move forward, sideways, or seemingly backward without first understanding why God is placing me there. God demanded Ezekiel to first seek out and then to speak up.

I recently met a dear friend for lunch. She recounted how all summer long she had been on her face before the Lord asking Him where He wanted her to serve now that she was a new empty nester. I was floored at what she then told me about the call God had for her. Her church was starting up a new ministry to combat inner-city sex trafficking. They would open a safe house where victims could be fed and clothed, where they would learn new skills so they could get off the street and support themselves, and most important, would learn about Christ. Now,

I can only speak for myself, but I find it most unlikely God would call me to such a ministry if my habit was to devote five quick minutes scanning through a chapter in my Bible followed by a seven-minute prayer. Why? Not because God couldn't do it, but because the idea of going to downtown Los Angeles and walking the streets befriending women who had been through some very tough stuff would scare me to death. Instead, it would take serious time before the Lord, bringing before Him my fears, listening to Him speak to me through His Word, and receiving all He said in my heart before my scaredy-cat selfishness would be pierced through to respond to Him in such radical obedience!

If you're floundering, wondering what it is the Lord might have for you, do what my friend did. No quick to-do list for her. Get down on your face before the Lord. Seek Him daily in the Scriptures. And this study is a great place to start!

READ EZEKIEL 3:12–16.

List the emotions Ezekiel experiences after this vision.

For how long did Ezekiel sit and process all he had seen and heard?

God asked Ezekiel to do something very difficult. He hinted that the results might be minimal. We don't actually know what Ezekiel is thinking, but in my humanness, I imagine it might sound something like this: *Really, God? Isn't it bad enough that I've already been exiled, taken far away from home, stuck here with no purpose or future, and now on top of it, God, You are asking me to do this?*

I mean, try and think of ten people you know who would be ecstatic about this call on their lives!

Can't even think of two? Yeah, me neither!

No wonder he's bitter. He is going to suffer because of others' sin, namely, the sin of those he is now called to serve. He is called to bring them messages from God—think of it—because they had not been listening to God. Not an easy task.

I'm sure some of us can relate. We have had someone in our lives who refuses to listen to God, and their consequences spill over onto us and we feel like it's unfair. We become bitter and wonder why we should have to suffer because of someone else's sin or stupidity.

Want to witness the neon sign of God's will? When it goes beyond our emotional ability to do it, beyond our mental ability to conceive it, and beyond our spiritual ability to desire it, it's generally God's idea.

Ezekiel needed to 100 percent depend on God to fulfill this call on his life. If what God calls us to doesn't have a bit of hard, doesn't ruffle our feathers or go beyond logical understanding, then we might be tempted to serve in our own flesh. Difficulty demands dependence and that's where God sticks His servants—in a place desperate for His power to come through. We ought not ever serve our almighty God through feeble human wisdom or frail strength.

Can you think of a hard season of your life? Describe your dependence on God at that time.

I love God's patience with Ezekiel at the conclusion of this vision. He sat for seven days—the customary mourning period. Remember the scroll of lamenting, mourning, and woe? God allowed Ezekiel to process the incredible vision and call he experienced. Life for Ezekiel was about to dramatically change, even beyond the difficulty and suffering he had already endured the last five years.

READ EZEKIEL 3:16–21.

Paraphrase what you think God's message to Ezekiel's fellow exiles includes.

READ EZEKIEL 3:22–27.

How would Ezekiel know he was only speaking God's words and not his own?

READ JOHN 16:12–15.

Who else only speaks the words of God?

For all the times I've stuck my foot in my mouth, what a relief to be saved from my own tongue! Ezekiel never need wonder if the message on his heart was to be shared or kept silent. God would open his mouth or shut it.

One thing we know we are continually commanded to share is the message of the glorious gospel of grace. How serious are we about that? On a scale from 1 to 5, where do you most readily fall?

1	2	3	4	5

*Can't remember
the last time
I've shared*

*Every
chance
I get!*

Sharing the message of Jesus' salvation might feel too hard or unfair. We might grow afraid of messing up or facing rejection. But it's our calling. If you landed on number one or maybe number two, go back to the beginning of today's homework and follow the three steps God outlined for Ezekiel. The gospel ought to always be on the tip of our tongue!

A PICTURE PAINTS A THOUSAND WORDS

EZEKIEL 4

We have probably all heard that expression about a picture a thousand times. Have you ever processed the truth of it? In Phoenix there used to be an anti-drug campaign that displayed billboards along our freeways. One of them haunted me every time I saw it. A mother was sitting on a chair beaten to the point of being barely recognizable. The caption read: "My mother knows I'd never hurt her, but then she got in the way." I found the image so disturbing my stomach turned each time I passed by. Now, if I passed a billboard that merely read, "Don't take drugs, they make you violent," I doubt that would evoke the same emotional and physical response in me. But the bruised and battered mother sitting despondently pierces me right to the heart. We are visual creatures, and the images we rest our eyes on become stamped in our memory, eliciting emotions deep within.

Our Creator knows how visual we are; He made us that way. So, in order to get the exiles' attention, God doesn't tell Ezekiel to stand on the corner and talk at them. He is going to have Ezekiel paint a picture for them to capture their curiosity and evoke an emotional reaction.

READ EZEKIEL 4:1–17.

How many words does Ezekiel speak?

Describe the scene he constructs in verses 1–4.[3]

What did Ezekiel lying on his left side and then his right side symbolize?

What was Ezekiel to do with his arm while acting this out?

How was he to eat and drink while lying there?

What did God concede so that Ezekiel did not defile himself by eating food that was unlawful?

Okay, we thought the visions were weird and confusing! What in the world is happening here? Let me break down a few things to help us make sense of this. Ezekiel was to take a clay brick and erect siege ramps around it. The brick symbolized the city of Jerusalem, which would be under siege by Nebuchadnezzar and eventually burned to the ground. Interestingly, clay becomes stronger when placed under fire. God's message to the exiles included the promise of a future strength at the end of their punishment. Iron represented the strongest element. The Jewish people believed that nothing could ever match the strength of Jerusalem because the Lord Himself dwelt there. However, God says that Jerusalem will fall.

Now for the numbers. God claims that the sin of Israel began 390 years ago. Read 1 Chronicles 21:1–17 and note what sin David had committed 390 years before and how God felt about it.

This sin highlights a shift in David's thinking from a complete and utter dependence on the Lord to pride and self-sufficiency. Not only are these sins often difficult to detect in our lives, but we also live in a culture that applauds them. We tend to distance ourselves from needy people and prefer to gravitate toward those who seem to have it all together. We like to associate with success. Our natural bent is also to try and fix things on our own. We'll work out how to take care of this bill or juggle the new schedule, or we read self-help books to make our marriage better and hire tutors to help our children succeed in school. Not that any of those things are bad per se, but it's often after we've exhausted all of our own resources and knowledge that we turn to the Lord for help.

What is a relationship or area of your life you often find yourself trying to fix in your own strength?

Why do you think your actions might grieve the Lord?

How long was Ezekiel to lie on his side the second time?

These periods of judgment represent two different things. The 390 years represent the span of time Israel had claimed self-sufficiency apart from God. The forty years represented the length of time Judah would be punished for this. As we've noted, by this time in Israel's history, the nation of Israel had been split in two, with ten of the original twelve tribes now comprising Israel, the northern kingdom, and the other two tribes comprising the southern kingdom, Judah. The northern portion, Israel, had already been captured over a hundred years prior by the Assyrians. Only the southern kingdom of Judah remains an independent nation, although they paid heavy tribute to the Babylonian king. For forty years God planned to punish the nation of Judah.

Read Exodus 6:6 and note what God would accomplish with bared or outstretched arm:

READ DEUTERONOMY 4:32–35.

What would God prove to the nation of Israel by the work of His bared or outstretched arm?

God bared His arm to deliver His people out of captivity from Egypt. Now His bared arm would drive them into captivity to refine and strengthen them. His purpose however remained constant: that His people would know that He is the Lord. God will repeat this purpose to His people over fifty times throughout the messages of Ezekiel.

Remember how we started today saying that a picture paints a thousand words? God's message to the exiles runs contrary to their thinking. They believed Jerusalem would forever remain impenetrable and secure and that God would soon deliver the exiles back to their promised land in a dramatic defeat of Nebuchadnezzar. God conjures up a vivid word picture to snap them back into reality. Their thinking is faulty.

Before you close your study book today, pause and ask the Lord to show you where any faulty thinking has crept into your own life. Is there an area of pride or self-sufficiency where you have ceased to depend on the Lord for your care? Maybe you have allowed standards to slip and you have defiled yourself as Ezekiel cried out against to the Lord (4:14).

Are you:

Neglecting family?

Demonstrating financial irresponsibility?

Partnering with people with questionable commitments to the Lord's will for their lives?

Avoiding confrontation?

Turning a blind eye to sin?

Not speaking up for the truth?

Continuing to pursue an unhealthy or destructive habit?

God longs to purify His people and have them depend on Him for their care and provision. Let's not allow faulty thinking to creep in and require fire to strengthen and cleanse us, or punishment to bring us to repentance. Instead, let's ask God to search our hearts today and resolve to allow Him to deliver us from any cords of sin that have begun to entangle us. Revival starts with inviting the Holy Spirit to search our hearts and provide inner reflection.

AWAKENED TO REVIVAL

Knowing Our God &
Awakening Our Purpose

THE SWORD IN THE SIEGE

EZEKIEL 5

In the middle of Ezekiel's charades before the exiles, which lasted the span of over a year, this strange interlude occurs. Ezekiel is to shave his head and beard with a sword, take his hair and weigh it on scales, burn one-third of it, slash one-third of it with the sword, scatter one-third of it around and chase it with the sword, yet keep a very small amount tucked away within the folds of his garment to later throw into the fire. I'm not going to lie, if I had lived among Ezekiel, I probably would have taken the long way home from the market just to keep my kids away from him. This is all more than slightly strange. And yet, we are told that the elders among the captives came and sat before him in order to receive a word from the Lord. So, while his methods veered from the traditional, he still held believability as a messenger among the people.

READ EZEKIEL 5:1–17. *Fill in the chart below:*

SINS OF THE HOUSE OF ISRAEL	CONSEQUENCES THEY WILL SUFFER

God called Israel to be a light to the nations—a beacon of hope, of righteousness and goodness, pointing their neighbors to God and turning them away from the futility of idols. However, not only had Israel become like the surrounding nations, but her sin actually exceeded theirs.

The shaved head symbolized mourning and a commitment to purity, while the shaved beard symbolized disgrace and humiliation. Priests were forbidden to shave their beards (Lev. 21:5) so there is a two-fold message involved in Ezekiel's actions: the true worship of God no longer exists, and the Law had been desecrated by the people of Israel. God warned the people of Israel just how dire and depraved they could become living apart from God's Law.

READ LEVITICUS 26:23–33.

What had God warned the people would happen should they turn away from Him?

As a mother, reading this makes my stomach turn! It makes the anti-drug campaign billboard described last week seem like nothing! Why does God include such jolting warnings? We need to remember two things. First, part of the detestable practices that the Israelites performed included sacrificing their children in the fire to the god Molech. They burned their children in hopes of prosperity. Second, we humans are prone to disregard the depths of our depravity. We find it unthinkable that we could behave so horrifically, even though the news regularly informs us that hundreds of thousands of children around the world are currently enslaved and abused in sex-trafficking, and that millions of babies are aborted annually because people are told parenting is not a good choice for them. If we are honest with ourselves, humanity has not become more morally enlightened as brightly as we'd like to believe.

We have all heard the expression "The punishment should fit the crime." The sins of Israel had become so exceedingly great that God warned of His need to inflict punishment on them more severely than He had ever inflicted before and would ever do so again.

READ HEBREWS 12:4–11.

What is the purpose of God's discipline?

Look carefully at Ezekiel 5:15. What would this punishment communicate to the surrounding nations?

That word "warning" is the Hebrew word *musar*.[4] An English synonym could be "instruction." The concept evokes the idea that one eventually becomes educated and their behavior altered when the proper amount of training and correction are imposed—God's behavior modification therapy.

This word occurs dozens of times in the book of Proverbs alone. Let's take a look at some of the benefits we receive from heeding the Lord's *musar*.

Read Proverbs 2:1–15 and list as many benefits of His musar *as you can find.*

God does not punish us because He is some big meanie in the sky longing to exact revenge. His commands are for our good, because He knows that when we stray from them, natural consequences will occur. When left to our own humanity, we experience horrific depravity. God punishes us to instruct us and return our hearts back to Him. He saves us from ourselves. God's punishment upon us, however, is not solely about us. We are usually trying to figure out the one thing God is doing in our own lives and fail to see the ten thousand things He is doing around us. God's punishment of His people also provided the pathway for the surrounding nations to come under His care and protection. Israel's punishment proved God's power—He could bountifully bless and dreadfully discipline.

Do you remember the onset of Israel's sin? When David counted the fighting men. Look at David's answer to God regarding his consequence.

"Let me fall into the hand of the LORD, for his mercy is very great, but do not let me fall into the hand of man" (1 Chron. 21:13).

Dear one, the discipline of the Lord is so much more merciful than the condemnation of the world. Our God disciplines for our good, out of love, but the world criticizes, condemns, and shames. God's goal is restoration; the world's: debilitation. Is there something in your past for which you continue to walk in shame? Give it over to the Lord now, for His mercy is very great.

Can you recall a time when God allowed you to experience a natural consequence for a poor choice made?

Can you think of a time when God used a trial in your life to touch someone else?

Are you going through a trial now and wondering how God could possibly be using it to instruct others? Ask Him to build your trust that He will bring a greater purpose beyond it than your own suffering.

The destruction and devastation the Israelites experienced within the walls of Jerusalem developed from natural consequences of their depravity. God's punishment proclaimed warnings far beyond the walls of that wicked city.

He warned the exiles to repent.

He warned the surrounding nations to repent.

He warned future generations to walk in God's ways and be protected from sin.

Rather than suffer the sharp sword of discipline, let's commit ourselves to the pang of transformation.

Read 1 Peter 4:12–13. What will occur due to our trials when Christ's glory is revealed?

Let's not keep our past mistakes hidden in shame. Tell of God's discipline in your life, providing instruction to those around you. It is often the most ravaging trials that become revolutionary testimonies.

PRIDEFUL POSITIONS

EZEKIEL 6–7

When Jonathan and I were newly married, we led a small group for couples. Out of the eight couples, all of us had been married for five years or less, except Barb and Dave. They had a good twenty-five years under their belt and had walked through a death-defying experience, which left Dave in chronic pain. Someone had entered his job site and began shooting, hitting Dave and leaving his back and legs riddled with bullets and shrapnel. Nearly every doctor who has ever encountered him considers his recovery nothing short of a miracle.

Most weeks in our study Dave said very little. He would welcome each of us with a big bear hug and then sit in his recliner and listen as we discussed our lessons. Every once in a while, however, he spoke up. And each time he did, the room fell silent, because when Dave spoke, he always delivered a zinger that went straight to the heart. Staring death in the face and experiencing God's decision to leave you on earth a while longer changes a person.

I imagine by the time Ezekiel finally opens his mouth to speak, his fellow exiles pause to hear what he has to say.

READ EZEKIEL 6.

Write the phrase that God repeats four times in this chapter:

The Hebrew word for "know" is the word *yada*—and it includes both an experiential and relational component. To know God implies being in a relationship with Him, not merely to have factual knowledge about Him. This same term is used to describe the sexual union between husband and wife, implying a deep level of intimacy.[5]

The word "Lord" is the formal name of God: Yahweh. Sometimes swapped with Adonai or Jehovah, the meaning encompasses the fullness of all the names by which God refers to Himself. "Yahweh, then, is the name par excellence of Israel's God. As Yahweh he is a faithful covenant God who, having given his Word of love and life, keeps that Word by bestowing love and life abundantly on his own."[6]

To interpret God's repeated phrase as a euphemism of "Then *I'll* show you who is God!" is to miss God's heartbeat entirely. Rather, God pleads for a return to relationship. He desires the Israelites to experience His love and His abundant life as their tender, present God. Instead, they have rejected Him.

One of the most tragic things I have ever had to walk through was the death of my friend's firstborn son in a senseless automobile accident. He had been out with friends drinking, got into his convertible, hit a pothole in the road, lost control of the car, and flipped over. He was taken by ambulance to the local hospital, and there he remained on life support for four solid months until the hospital finally convinced his mom to let him go. My friend vacillated between deep grief and anger. Grief over the loss of her son and anger for his foolish choice that took him too soon and injured another young man for life. The process shattered her heart to pieces and she has never been the same. How could she be?

Such is Yahweh with His own: angered by our foolish rebellion, yet heart-wrenchingly grieved over the loss of relationship. He mourns the consequences it brings to our lives. God longs for us to live according to His commands that we might be spared devastation. Yet even when we wander, He pursues us to bring us back to Him. We are never too far away to return to the arms of our Father.

God continues to pour out His punishment in Ezekiel 7. *Look carefully at verses 10, 20, 24 and notice what word God repeats to describe their sin:*

_____

There is an important differentiation here between Israel and the surrounding nations. Israel's neighbors remained ignorant about what it meant to "know Yahweh." The people of Israel, however, deliberately misrepresented Him. The people of Israel wanted to show their neighbors how they were just like them instead of showing the world the incredible blessing of being in relationship with God. What we know and believe about God determines what kind of witness we will be. Does this relationship result in transformation on the inside that demonstrates a life of humility and service on the outside?

Instead, the Israelites became prideful over the blessings of their covenant relationship with God. Their money, their jewelry, their bountiful harvests, even the temple itself—all causes of pride. One of the surest ways to identify sources or areas of pride in our lives comes in moments of insecurity. What boosts our ego when we feel lower than the person next to us? To what do we cling when we feel the need to prove ourselves: our Instagram account, our bank accounts, our clothing size, some name dropping, our children's successes, a business card with all the letters and accolades, a jam-packed day planner demonstrating how important we are to so many and how capable of juggling the impossible?

God called Israel to be His treasured people, and this alone gave Israel her great worth. God desired Israel to know Him experientially and relationally, and to share that knowledge with her neighboring nations.

Nothing differs with us. Our worth resides in our relationship with Christ. God's desire is that we may know Christ fully and make Him fully known. No other call is greater. There is nothing of more importance than this. Just because your boss, your sister, your friend, or your neighbor does not believe it, that doesn't make it any less true.

Who are you showing Christ to in your life?

We get the idea that God takes knowing Him pretty seriously. And He takes His call to show others who He is pretty seriously. The people of Israel have not taken either one very seriously. So, what is the result? God lays out some pretty harsh consequences. If we are wise, we will examine them closely and heed His warnings.

According to Ezekiel 7:26, what would the people no longer have?

According to Ezekiel 7:27, by what standards would they be judged?

This is such a profound commentary on pride. The people could no longer receive instruction from the Lord. The prophets' visions ceased, the Lord's word grew silent. The leaders' wisdom failed them. Nothing clouds our ability to receive instruction and lead objectively like pride. Notice also, this horrific judgment of which God warned equaled the judgment they poured out on their neighbors. They saw the surrounding nations as sinful and themselves righteous. Pride hides our sin and clouds our view: especially our internal one.

Back when I taught elementary school, we'd start each year with the creation of our class rules. These rules would be decided on collaboratively with guidance by me as their teacher. Once the rules had been decided, we would get to the consequences. The children were always so much harder on each other than I ever would be! I would ask, "Class, suppose one of our members chooses not to abide by one of these rules we have agreed on, what do you think should happen?" Their answers made me laugh. No recess for a month. Send them to the principal. Make them eat lunch against the wall alone. Call their parents. Because children are prideful, it does not occur to them that most likely every single one of them would interrupt, talk out of turn, get out of their seat, or say something unkind to one another at some point during the school year. An inability to recognize our own propensity toward sin is indeed childish, and a sure sign of spiritual immaturity.

Instead of God intervening and showing mercy, He agreed to inflict the harsh punishment the Israelites wished to be imposed on their neighbors on themselves. By their own standards God would judge them.

Want another quick pride check? What do you wish on those you view as evil? That they would return to God and live? Or suffer a horrible end?

I have a friend who often says, "Look in the mirror, not out the window!" Let's ask God to search within us and reveal any areas of pride that have unknowingly crept in. Nothing halts revival like a lack of humility.

MARKED

EZEKIEL 8–9

Ezekiel concludes his 430 days of lying on his sides, acting out a siege, barely eating and drinking a thing, and speaking only twice. Suddenly he packs up his mini-theater and returns home. The people must be curious! What does this mean? Has God changed His mind regarding the prophecies against Jerusalem? The exiles have been in Babylon six years now with presumably little to no word regarding their beloved homeland.

READ EZEKIEL 8:1–6.

Who goes to inquire of the Lord through Ezekiel?

Describe the "man" Ezekiel sees.

How is Ezekiel transported in this vision, and where is he taken?

What does Ezekiel see in the inner court?

What does God claim the people are causing Him to do? (v. 6)

Now part of this vision just cracks me up! At least we know Ezekiel's hair has grown back over the last 430 days. I get the idea that maybe Ezekiel became swept into this vision reluctantly. I can't blame him. He's just finished a tough 430 days and finally got to go home! Who knows what he's going to have to do next!

Ezekiel is taken within the walls of the city of Jerusalem. The north gate of the altar means he is within the temple itself and notices the "image of jealousy," which likely refers to an idol, such as one erected under the direction of King Manasseh (see 2 Kings 21:1–3).

READ EZEKIEL 8:7–17.

How many of Judah's elders did Ezekiel see secretly worshiping idols?

What name does he include among them?

What do these elders claim about God?

Let's get to know this elder a little more intimately.

READ 2 KINGS 22:1–20.

Who is the king of Judah here, and how is he described?

Who is Shaphan, and how did he respond when the Book of the Law was found?

What does Josiah do after he hears the Book of the Law, and what instructions does he give to Shaphan?

King Josiah spent the remainder of his reign systematically eradicating idol worship from the land of Judah under the supervision of Shaphan, his secretary. Josiah reigned as king until 609 BC and Ezekiel became exiled in 597 BC, merely twelve years later. Shaphan's son, Jaazaniah, just one generation later, walked away from his father's faithful devotion to God and embraced idol worship. This scene no doubt proved jolting to Ezekiel as well as the elders who sat before him. How could a devout and faithful man's son turn to such wickedness?

God's response to this blatant idolatry in His temple comes next. Warning: some of this may prove difficult to read. We don't spend much time absorbing God's punishment of evil in our modern-day churches. Its purpose is jolting. These vivid pictures of sin serve to revolt us against the pervasive consequences of sin spilling over onto those who surround us. This prophetic vision provides a picture of Jesus issuing judgment upon those who refuse to repent of their idolatry, allowing God's people to understand the future work and role of their Messiah. Our tendency will be to see this judgment as excessively harsh rather than an attempt to open our eyes to the reality of sin's grievousness. God's desire is to get our attention and pierce our heart.

READ EZEKIEL 9:1–11.

What was the man in linen commanded to do?

Who were the first to be killed?

What did Ezekiel cry out to the Lord?

How did God respond?

Biblical scholar Charles Feinberg explains, "From His clothing and the nature of the work He is seen to accomplish later, it is to be inferred that the Chief of the company was the Angel of the Lord, the preincarnate Christ."[7] ("Preincarnate" refers to an appearance of Christ before His birth as a human being.) Christ marked His own—those who grieved over the sin of the people and their loss of love for God. Ezekiel witnessed the elders slain first—those who held the responsibility to lead the people and teach them the command of the Lord. Notice Ezekiel's response, however. He has just witnessed these leaders doing the unthinkable and accusing God of forgetting and forsaking them. Yet still he cries out in intercession!

READ JEREMIAH 2:26–28.

What does Jeremiah, a contemporary of Ezekiel, claim the people in Jerusalem were saying in verses 26–27?

How often do we go our own way, do our own thing, and then complain when God doesn't shield us from the consequences of our obstinacy? We want God to leave us alone, until we've backed ourselves into a corner or crossed a circumstance beyond our control. Then we cry out and wonder why He doesn't immediately swoop in to save us. Does that mean God is apathetic, unable, unjust, or untruthful when He promised to never leave us or forsake us? Quite the opposite!

If God continually warned us of the consequences of sin, yet never allowed us to experience them, then we would have to question His truthfulness. Rather, He makes the consequences abundantly clear in His Word and allows us to choose. Remember, this is a *prophetic* vision. Jeremiah remains within the city imploring them to repent and Christ remains faithful to mark His own to be spared. The people have a choice—turn to God and live, or continue to worship idols.

What will mark our generation? Will we be seen as Christ's own, longing to remain His pure church, or will we collapse under cultural pressure, chasing comfort and prosperity?

A LONG GOODBYE

EZEKIEL 10

It was the third evening of sitting at my father's bedside. I desperately needed a shower and a decent night's sleep, but I knew I would never make it back early enough to be there for his short morning rally. So, I folded my pillow in half over the wooden arm of the chair and closed my eyes. As always, my father woke up with the first light of the sun. Even on his deathbed. For maybe twenty minutes or less each morning, he'd emerge from his listless sleep and speak to me. I wanted every last moment with him I could experience—more than anything else in the world.

If you've ever walked with someone until their last breath, you know. That desperate desire to hold on and not let go. Somehow you think that if you hold their hand tightly enough maybe they'll stay just a little longer—there will be one more conversation, one last memory forged.

In today's passage, God lingered in the midst of His people. They rejected His glory, pushed Him away, and embraced idolatry. They slandered His commitment to His promises and yet He still hesitated. His heart pierced over His departure. The portion of Ezekiel's vision we will cover today paints one of the most beautiful pictures of God's heart—even in judgment—recorded in Scripture.

READ EZEKIEL 10:1–18.

Based on Ezekiel's previous vision, which place can we conclude Ezekiel is visualizing?

What was the man in linen instructed to do?

Where was the glory of the Lord originally and where did it go next? (See especially vv. 3–4).

What does Ezekiel make sure we understand in verse 18?

The man in linen—who is likely the preincarnate Christ—marked those who longed for God's glory to remain among them. Now in the time of judgment, Ezekiel cried out in desperation when God began to prophesy the punishment and destruction that would come upon his fellow Israelites within the walls of Jerusalem. What happens in verse 3 holds the most significance. The cloud symbolizes the presence of the Lord. Initially He is in the Holy of Holies, His predetermined position in the temple. God, however, exits the Holy of Holies and travels to the inner court. He is departing from His dwelling place.

READ EZEKIEL 10:18–22.

Where does the glory of the Lord go next?

Through which gate did God's glory pass?

The Scripture says the glory "stood" at this gate (v. 18), that is, stood still. The New International Version says "stopped above." I want you to process this fully. Ezekiel witnesses the enactment of God's judgment upon His people. Yet, at the moment of final separation, God paused. He stopped at the gate. Think about it: God did not storm out of the temple ranting how this rebellious city stood undeserving of His presence. He stopped at the gate. He lingered. His heart still longed to remain in the presence of His people and restore relationship with them despite their rejection of Him. After all of their accusations against Him, their defiance and rebellion toward Him, He stopped at the gate.

READ MATTHEW 23:37–38.

What does this passage show us about Jesus' heart toward the people of Jerusalem?

These are the same people who would mock Him, ridicule Him, and hand Him over to be tortured and crucified. But He weeps for them. That is the problem with sin: it clouds our vision and doesn't allow us to realize the level of confusion, deception, and destruction it brings to our lives. The people accused God of deserting them, but it was the people who insisted on pushing Him away.

I'll never forget the day my friend Faith shared her testimony at Bible study:

> I got the call in the middle of the night. That was always a bad sign. My daughter Terri was on the other end of the phone weeping, begging me to come pick her up. It always went like that. Jim and I would drive downtown to some hellhole or another and drag her out and bring her home. A few days later she'd disappear

again. Then her twins were born and the agony exponentially tripled. She'd pull it together for a while and try to be a good mom, but it never lasted. She'd go back to her so-called boyfriend. Every time. The battle to open our daughter's eyes to the captivity of her relationship felt like a losing fight. Now we had two grandchildren caught in the snare as well.

It was early morning as I pulled up in front of the dilapidated house. My grandson recognized my car, bolted through the screen door hanging on by one hinge, and sprinted toward me. I couldn't even unbuckle my seat belt and open the door before he stood there crying and pounding on the door. Terri came out slowly, barely able to walk. This beating was the worst I'd seen. My granddaughter clung to her mom's leg and I could see my daughter wince at her touch.

I got them all into the car. All their possessions fit inside one black plastic trash bag. It seemed to be such a fitting picture of their life—cast aside, devalued, and disregarded. "I'm hungry, Grammy!" my grandson whimpered. I took them through the McDonald's drive-through and my grandbabies eagerly devoured their biscuits and eggs. My daughter sat in silence. As I drove past the highway exit to our home, she finally spoke. "Mom, where are you going? You were supposed to get off back there." This time it was I who remained silent.

"Mom, where are we going?" my daughter demanded. "Home," I stammered. She was clearly confused and said nothing else. Five minutes later I pulled into the driveway of the women's shelter. "Oh, no, no, no!" my daughter wailed. "You are *not* taking me here! This is *not* where I belong! How could you even think of letting your grandchildren live in a place like this?" The question stung. How could I, indeed. I knew she couldn't come home. The cycle would never break as long as home remained an option. I opened the car door and she trembled as she got out.

My own hands trembled as I held on to the car door handle to steady myself. A beautiful woman emerged from the porch with suckers for the children and big hugs. She came and put her arm around my daughter's shoulder, turned her around, and guided her into the house. My grandbabies smiled at me, holding up their suckers, and followed their mother, eyes shining with happiness over their round red treats. I slumped back down into the driver's seat. My hands trembled violently as I tried to put my key into the ignition. Tears poured down my cheeks, muddying my view. I didn't know if I actually had the strength to go through with this even though I knew that it was the only way my daughter and grandchildren had any chance at a restored life.

God knew His people needed to experience the consequences of their idolatry to turn them around and lead them back to relationship with Him. God's warnings and former attempts to recapture their hearts remained lost on them. This was the only way to restore life.

Faith gratefully showed us photos of her daughter and grandchildren. As those of us around the table could see, the children were thriving—doing well in school and involved in church and school activities. Terri had completed her nursing degree and was able to provide a good living for her family. A trio of incredible faith and service to Christ and a testimony of God's restorative power. Terri said, "That day marked the turning point of my life. I knew my mom and dad could not save me, only God could. And finally, for the first time in my life as I sat down on my bed in the women's shelter, I ran *to* Him instead of from Him. I came home."

God did not leave nor forsake His people. He merely allowed them to experience the devastating consequences of sin. Reluctantly, He lingered, hoping for any other way to recapture their hearts.

Is there an area of your heart bowing down to an idol? It's time to lay it on the altar and come home. God has not left you—He is right there waiting with open arms.

I KNOW WHAT YOU'RE THINKING

EZEKIEL 11

We left off yesterday right in the middle of Ezekiel's latest vision depicting God's departure from the temple in Jerusalem and His judgment on the city. The glory of God moved from within the Holy of Holies, to the inner court, the edge of the temple mount, and then stopped at the east gate. Here is where the vision continues.

READ EZEKIEL 11:1–13.

Who does Ezekiel see there?

What does the Lord hear them doing?

What advice are they giving to the people?

What did the Lord say He hears and knows?

Whom does God state to be the cauldron and the meat?

What was God's purpose in bringing judgment upon them? What would they "know"? (v. 10)

Whose "rules" were these men following?

Outside of the east gate, merchants set up shop to sell their wares. The elders also sat at the gates. Because Ezekiel immediately recognizes two of them and mentions them by name, we can presume these guys are the rich and famous of their day. This Jaazaniah is not the same as the previous one mentioned in chapter 8, as this one is the son of Azzur, not of Shaphan the royal secretary. It is interesting that Ezekiel mentions very few men by name in his visions, yet two Jaazaniahs! What is even more interesting is what the name means: The LORD hears.

God's people in Jerusalem complained that the Lord did not see their tribulation as vassals of Nebuchadnezzar. God ups the ante and basically says, "Oh, I see all right! And I hear too! I even know what you're thinking!" These leaders considered the exiles to be the recipients of the Lord's punishment and wrath, while they remained unscathed. Referring to Jerusalem as the cauldron and themselves the meat greatly speaks to their pride. A cauldron is an impenetrable iron pot. When you made a stew, the tastiest and most valuable ingredients included the meat. These guys were the top dogs of the city. They promised prosperity and a bright future to the people. The exact opposite of what their prophet Jeremiah warned against.

The king of Babylon conquered surrounding nations and then kept the country's previous king on the throne. The king became Nebuchadnezzar's vassal, allowing him to maintain his position of power, but requiring him to pay expensive tribute to Babylon. Instead of the people returning to God in repentance, these twenty-five men decided they were better off exploiting the current situation. They conformed to the idolatrous surrounding nations worshiping worldly wealth and power rather than living holy lives for God.

If we are honest, our culture is not too much different today. Even the church.

If we were to poll one hundred Christian women and ask them to name twenty-five media celebrities or twenty-five biblical principles or Scripture verses from memory, which task do you think would be easier for most to complete? Why do you think so? Write your opinion below:

We have got to get to a place where we are serious about knowing God's Word. God warned Ezekiel in this vision that the time would come when the people would seek the Word of the Lord but it would not be found. Are we committed to feeding on God's Word (Ezek. 3:3) as God commanded Ezekiel?

What are some areas where you see the world's standards infiltrating the church?

READ 1 THESSALONIANS 5:23–24.

What is Paul's prayer for the Christians in Thessalonica?

Look closely at verse 24. On whom do we rely to keep us holy?

This prayer of Paul directly reflects God's plans for the exiles.

READ EZEKIEL 11:14–25.

What is being said by the people still in Jerusalem regarding the exiles?

What does God say He will do for the exiles? (see v. 17)

What will the exiles do in return? (see v. 18)

How do verses 19–20 echo Paul's prayer over the church in Thessalonica?

Isn't that just like our God? He doesn't just restore, He does abundantly more! He doesn't just bring them home, He brings them into relationship with Himself, giving them a new heart and a new spirit within them! The glory of God that dwelt within the hidden darkness of the temple now resides within the soul of man! Astounding! He doesn't just take away our sinfulness, He fills us with His righteousness. Praise Him for His abundant goodness!

Those of us who "know He is the Lord God"—who have experienced His goodness—find it hard to understand why some would reject God's offer of relationship. But God firmly states that there are those who prefer to go after their idols (v. 21).

Which will we be? The biggest question I had at the end of this vision is—and Ezekiel does not tell us—how did the people respond? I mean, here God promises they will return home, their nation will be restored, He is still their God and they are still His people, and He will give them a new, undivided heart. Those are some pretty big promises! Yet, we are not informed of their response.

Maybe God's not so interested in having us understand the response of the ancients. Maybe today, He'd prefer to discuss ours. God sees, hears, and knows what we are thinking. Will we return to Him, allowing Him to sanctify us? Or will we chase after the things of this world? Revival starts with us.

THE TRUTH REGARDING REVIVAL

Let the Truth Be Told

CAN YOU GIVE ME A SIGN, PLEASE?

EZEKIEL 12

Have you ever traveled to a foreign country where you could not read or understand the native language at all? My first experience happened in Germany. My husband and I boarded a train from Stuttgart to Neuchwanstein and sat down. A few minutes into the ride a man came by and spoke to us in German. I looked back at him and muttered, "English, American," as I was not sure what else to say. He repeated the same phrase again at me in German only this time more loudly. I shook my head and shrugged my shoulders. He then yelled the phrase and began gesturing at me violently. Whatever he was trying to communicate remained lost on me. Finally, a young man across the aisle leaned over and said, "Madam, he needs to see your ticket!" He could have yelled and gestured for the entire train ride and I'm not sure I ever would have gotten the message. This seemed to be the case with Ezekiel's audience as well.

Thus far, Ezekiel demonstrated some strange gestures of his own, yet the people still do not understand God's plan for them or for the people who remain in

Jerusalem. So, this go-around, Ezekiel will not only gesture, he will also speak. God is going to lean across the aisle and try and spell things out for them a bit more clearly.

READ EZEKIEL 12:1–16.

What charade did Ezekiel play out?

What explanation did he give as to its meaning?

When the captives initially saw Ezekiel packing his bags, what might they have hoped he meant? (Revisit Ezekiel 11:16–17.)

I think God wanted to make sure they didn't get any wrong ideas when they saw suitcases. Their train ticket to head back home was not being issued any time soon. God had other plans. More exiles would soon be joining them, including their very own King Zedekiah.

READ EZEKIEL 12:17–28.

What did God say will happen to the city of Jerusalem?

What will the captives know as a result?

What proverb did the people quote indicating their ideas that this would not happen until a time far off?

How did God respond to this thinking?

Doesn't that sound so much like us in our day? We take God's words and insist they mean only future blessings and leave out the demands for obedience. Or we rationalize and say, "Well, okay, maybe God is asking us for some level of obedience here, but He doesn't really mean it. It's figurative." Then once we are forced to concede that God actually does warn of judgment, we casually shrug our shoulders and say, "Sure, God will judge sin, but not for a long time off, so I don't really need to worry about it today!" And all the while God attempts to spark revival within us while we discount His warnings. It's almost as if God is responding to these rationalizations of the exiles in real time right as the thoughts roll around in their heads.

Do you remember the Disney classic *Pinocchio*?[8] This reminds me of the part when Pinocchio is on Pleasure Island and Jiminy Cricket is warning him that something bad will soon happen. Jiminy does not know exactly what, so he cannot issue Pinocchio any specifics, but he knows something bad is brewing. The rebellious Lampwick insists there is nothing to fear, but before he even finishes his emphatic assertion, two donkey ears pop out of his head and a tail springs from his backside. Pinocchio looks on in horror as Lampwick begins to bray like a donkey and is no longer able to speak. For every word of advice Jiminy Crickett so desperately tried to get Pinocchio to hear, he had been drowned out by Lampwick, who refuted every word. Now, however, Lampwick is finally silenced and all he can do is bray!

From Ezekiel 12:24, we learn that other prophets were speaking to the exiled in Babylon but Ezekiel was speaking the truth of God and warning them of impending judgment. Others were false prophets, interested only in flattery. Ezekiel's call to repentance remained drowned out by those who preached peace and prosperity for Israel.

Why is it that we wait to witness the fulfillment of God's Word in living color in front of us before we finally believe Him? Do we need to see people before our very eyes reaping what they have sown before we will humble our hearts and bend the knee in repentance? God knew that it was not until the city of Jerusalem crumbled that the exiles would finally acknowledge Him as Lord, their covenant-keeping God who would fulfill His promises both inside and outside the confines of the Holy City. (See Ezekiel 12:20.)

How about you and me? Is there someone or something we are listening to who is leading us to complacency? Where is our Pleasure Island and who is our Lampwick? These may be good people, but they are just not as focused on the things of God as we strive to be. Remnants of the world continue to allure them.

God warned His people continually against false teachers who would sow seeds of doubt as to whether God would truly keep His promises of correction and consequences.

READ 2 PETER 3:3–14.

What question will scoffers ask?

What is the reason for God delaying His coming?

How then are we to live?

What will result in our living this way?

God's plan of salvation and day of His return are determined and known only by Him. Through His death and resurrection on the cross, Christ secured our salvation. God now delays His judgment on the earth so that more may come to repentance. He desires that none perish. How is this salvation plan made increasingly plain for the world to see? Through the testimony of transformed lives that are spotless, blameless, and at peace.

If our lives were truly lived in surrender to Christ, and thus transformed by the power of His Holy Spirit within us, could a scoffer say, "All things are continuing as they were from the beginning"? I pray not! If our lives look the same as they did before we received Christ's salvation, then we need to prayerfully consider this question of Peter: "What sort of people ought you to be?" Our lives ought to reflect the transforming power of the grace given us, because this is how others are able to see Christ in us, the hope of glory!

Confess to the Lord today any area of your life He shows you that needs His transforming touch of grace. Ask Him for the grace to believe in His power to change your life and become a living testimony to the power of His salvation. Pray for revival: an inward change in your heart that results in an outward change in your behavior. Write a prayer of commitment to follow Him in obedience to whatever He shows you.

LET THE TRUTH BE TOLD

EZEKIEL 13

We discovered yesterday that Ezekiel stood as one of many prophets among his people. However, he appears to be the only true messenger of God among the exiles. Jeremiah, as mentioned, a contemporary of Ezekiel, prophesied God's Words to those still in Jerusalem. He, too, preached of impending doom and destruction of the city of Jerusalem and was equally disbelieved by his people. Even today we are surrounded by many who claim to be preaching a Christian message but seem to slip in a few ideas that contradict traditional biblical interpretation. We must commit to knowing the Word of God and studying it diligently so that we might test everything against Scripture at all times.

For what did Paul commend the Bereans in Acts 17:11?

READ EZEKIEL 13:1–4.

To what did God equate the false prophets of Ezekiel's day?

Since I am the world's biggest city slicker you will ever meet, I am always intrigued by these references where God equates humans to animal-like behavior. A jackal is a wild dog (translated "fox" in some versions) known for its slyness and trickery. A natural predator, a jackal forages for food. The false prophets preyed on the exiles who already endured captivity, to extract as much from them as they could.

Let's think about present times. What kind of person would you consider a false prophet today? How can you recognize a false prophet?

READ EZEKIEL 13:5–16.

What should the prophets have implored the people to do?

Can you think of some "breaches" or gaps within our churches today, areas where there is work to be done? What are some societal issues that the church is facing today that demand courage to tackle? One term that comes to mind is "deconstruction," which is a term that refers to doubting and likely rejecting the tenets of the Christian faith. More often than not this process leads, not to honest exploring of the faith or working through questions, but to people turning away from their faith communities and even denigrating the church. What are some other examples you can think of?

Rather than dealing with the cracks or breaches, what did the people choose to do instead?

What message did the false prophets deliver? How would this lead the people to complacency in regard to the condition of the wall?

What prophecy did God issue regarding the wall, and what would the people know as a result?

In ancient times, city walls provided protection against attackers. The height of the walls included tall towers in which scouts positioned themselves to keep watch over the city and sound warnings against possible invaders approaching from afar. A solid wall meant the difference between having peace and safety or being plagued by assault and strife. If you are picturing a castle in your mind, you get the idea. But instead of repairing the breaches in the crumbling walls, they coated the cracks with whitewash to disguise the wall's weakness. God paints a picture using a tangible object, the walls of Jerusalem, to teach a harsh truth regarding Israel's spiritual condition. The people allowed dangerous ideas and idolatry to seep into their holy city, and these philosophies and beliefs now penetrated their hearts.

We cannot build our faith and our churches on flimsy walls of half-truths, half-hearted obedience, picking and choosing those portions of Scripture that we like to make into beautiful memes on Instagram or T-shirts and coffee mugs, while conveniently forgetting the hard truths Christ commands us to obey.

Consider these words of David Platt:

> We take Jesus' command in Matthew 28 to make disciples of all nations and we say, "That means other people." But we look at Jesus' command in Matthew 11:28, "Come to me, all you who are weary and burdened and I will give you rest," and we say, "Now that means me." We take Jesus' promise in Acts 1:8 that the Spirit will lead us to the ends of the earth, and we say, "That means some people." But we take Jesus' promise in John 10:10 that we will have abundant life, and we say, "That means me." In the process we have unnecessarily (and unbiblically) drawn a line of distinction, assigning the obligations of Christianity to a few, while keeping the privileges of Christianity for us all.[9]

If we want rock-solid faith, the peace, rest, and abundant life Jesus promised, we must ask the Holy Spirit to prepare our hearts to receive all of Christ's commands with courage to follow Him in complete obedience. We cannot cover our sinfulness with whitewash, nor can we cease asking the Holy Spirit to survey the stones on which we ardently stand. We cannot downplay sinful areas of our lives where we continue to walk in our own way and expect Christ to just gloss over it because He knows we are sinners. The people in Ezekiel's day only wanted to hear of God's protection and blessing. They held no interest in being confronted with their sin that they might turn in repentance and receive God's promised revival.

When is the last time you experienced the Lord's conviction in your life? Not the kind of guilt that comes from comparing yourself to someone else, but the Spirit of conviction in response to your reading of Scripture?

If you are rarely being challenged through the teaching of your pastor or your study of God's Word, you may need to examine the walls of your heart. We need to receive admonishment as well as encouragement! A dead giveaway of a false prophet is someone who continually preaches "peace" and never warns of the storms (Ezek. 13:11–12). Remember, these false prophets existed for many years within the nation of Israel before God brought His judgment on them. We cannot merely look at outward signs of success in our modern-day churches and assume that the hearts of the leaders are committed to preaching the Word of the Lord in its entirety. Only when we study the Scriptures diligently ourselves will we be able to discern when the walls of our hearts are being whitewashed with platitudes of peace and comfort, yet neglecting the hammer of conviction, testing our resolve.

Once a wall became breached, destruction proved imminent. The enemy had effectively penetrated the obstacle that kept him from unabated attack. When attackers sought to invade a city, they intentionally studied the city walls to find previous breaches, searching for points of weakness where they could easily penetrate. If a wall suffered too many breaches, its only hope of refortification became the wall's entire destruction, thus beginning the arduous task of rebuilding on its original foundation again. Can you see the connection spiritually? Our enemy studies the walls of our heart to find the easiest entry points. To repair a breach, the exposed section of the wall must be filled with something, not merely washed over while the gaping hole remains. We must ask the Holy Spirit to fill our hearts completely. We choose to surrender over to Him in obedience as He brings conviction to areas of our heart that are yet weak and unwilling to obey Christ's Word fully.

READ MATTHEW 7:21–27.

These words of Jesus prove difficult. What two things does Jesus claim will ensure our house is being built on a rock?

We cannot put into practice what we don't know, and we must live what we have been taught. The wall around the city of Jerusalem, which included the temple, exemplified the people's security, just as the Word of the Lord and Christ's commands and promises are ours. Are we solely depending on the teaching of others to remind us of our security and gazing on whitewashed walls, or are we doing the hard labor of building up the strength of the wall of our hearts by committing to learn and live by the truths of Scripture? Do we sit idly by waiting for our salvation, or do we work diligently asking the Holy Spirit in our study of the Word to shine His light on any cracks in the wall and subsequently repair them?

What imagery did Jesus use to describe the people's rejection of Him coming as their promised King in Luke 19:41–44?

Our enemy studies the walls of our heart. He searches for breaches. Will we invite God to do His repair work filling those gaps with the greatness of His Word?

How would you rate your commitment to the study of Scripture?

1	5	10
I could go days without reading my Bible and not miss it	*I try to spend some time each day reading*	*I have treasured the words of His mouth more than my daily bread*

Ask the Lord to fill you with a desire for His Holy Word. Commit to spending time daily in it, to know Him through it. The Master Builder longs to do some repair work in our hearts. He longs to fill those empty, gaping holes with newness of life and strength through the truth and testing of our thoughts by His Word.

LET THE TRUTH BE TOLD, CONTINUED

EZEKIEL 13

While on vacation our family encountered the rare treat of shopping at a Christian bookstore. When we returned to our car, we found a pamphlet stuffed into our door jamb inviting us to have our future told by a local psychic. I then proceeded to remove the pamphlets from several of the vehicles in the parking lot and fortunately didn't set off any car alarms. Have I ever mentioned that sometimes I react to things without thinking them all the way through?

The deception angered me and it also struck me as so odd that the psychic would market herself specifically to people shopping at a Christian bookstore. I thought, "Surely she would know that people spending their money on Christian literature find their hope in the Word of God and not a crystal ball or a deck of cards!" But maybe the opposite is true. Maybe some people shopping at a Christian bookstore *are* concerned over their future and are eagerly seeking answers to some deep questions, and the psychic preys on this, looking for people who haven't yet discovered the truth of God's Word. These shoppers are willing to spend time and money in search of the answers they seek.

Such was the case in Ezekiel's day. The captives were desperate for answers as to what the future held for them, and some of the daughters of Jerusalem cashed in on their insecurity. They used ancient practices of incantation and fortune-telling.

READ EZEKIEL 13:17–23.

What does the Lord accuse these women of doing? (See especially verse 19.)

What would the Lord do for His people in regard to these false diviners, and what would they know as a result?

What effect were these women having on the righteous?

I want to examine the plight of the captives from God's perspective for a moment. The people received false prophecies from their prophets and priests. They further employed those practicing divination for direction for their lives, which stood in stark opposition to God's Laws for His people. In other words, they grasped at anything for a sense of security except for surrender to God. In the midst of this scrambling, God speaks regarding the disheartening of the righteous. Let's explore that a bit more intently. To profane something is to invite something secular into the midst of the sacred. It also includes treating something sacred disrespectfully.

Have you seen our churches today inviting the secular into the midst of the sacred? In what way(s)? How might we treat God's holiness and commands disrespectfully?

The righteous remained disheartened because people were being comforted rather than confronted. These false prophets and prophetesses were being warned to turn from their evil ways; they sang songs of peace causing the people to continue in their complacency. Anytime we are listening to the Word of God being taught and we are not encouraged to follow in surrender, realizing the great gap between God's holiness and our feeble humanity, our ears ought to perk up and we should ask the Spirit for discernment.

When we begin to say things like, "I have enough hard truth from Scripture I am struggling to obey. I can't handle any more!" we must fall on our faces before God in surrender and ask for grace and mercy to help us in our time of need. Our purpose in attending a worship service on Sunday isn't so we feel better—the purpose is invite God to transform us. Sometimes transformation can get a little uncomfortable and at other times downright painful! I am so grateful to attend a church where my pastor is more committed to my holiness than my happiness. It is far more important to him that I know and believe the Lord than I walk out on a Sunday morning musing over what a great message he delivered.

A difficult reality remains. Jesus' commands far exceed our ability to obey them. Does that mean Jesus was not serious in His requests? Far from it! Those commands cite our breaches in the walls of our hearts and our need for the strong hands of fortification that only Jesus can provide. It also invites us to breathe a sigh of relief that we have been filled with the Holy Spirit until Jesus' return.

Read 1 Peter 1:3–5 and fill in the blanks:

Blessed be the God and Father of our Lord Jesus Christ! According to his great mercy, he has caused us to be born again to a living hope through the resurrection of Jesus Christ from the dead, to an inheritance that is _____, _____, and _____, kept in heaven for you, who by _____ through faith for a salvation ready to be revealed in the last time.

Exactly how are we kept and guarded? By the power of God through faith. Not by trying harder. Grunting it out. Beating ourselves up. Ruminating in guilt and shame. We hold fast to faith in God's power to keep us secure, safe, and steadfast. And how do we enrich our faith in this power? Ah dear one, through His Word. Through truth. And asking in faith for the Wonderful Counselor to illuminate it and apply it to our lives in all of its mighty power. Andrew Murray said,

> The cause of the weakness of your Christian life is that you want to work it out partly, and to let God help you. And that cannot be. You must come to be utterly helpless, to let God work, and God will work gloriously. It is this that we need if we are indeed to be workers for God.[10]

The captives of Ezekiel's day sought direction as to what they could do. They insisted knowing their future would help them prepare for it, manipulate it, or somehow secure a more favorable outcome than the fate their Father deemed for them. Our good and perfect Father holds our future. Oh, fellow believer, examine again closely what future awaits us: our glorious inheritance in heaven that cannot be taken from us. Hallelujah! Let us not insist on knowing what tomorrow holds, but let's hold on to the One who holds tomorrow. He will keep us and guard us. He holds the answer to every question we seek.

Sit before the Lord today and talk to Him regarding what concerns you most about the future. Acknowledge His ability to guard and protect you and the inheritance that awaits you due to Christ's death and resurrection!

THE ANSWERS WE SEEK

EZEKIEL 14

Have you ever met those people who, in the sudden wake of great difficulty or loss, finally turn to the Lord? They have lived their lives their own way, doing their own thing, but once faced with something so large they desperately need miraculous intervention or divine wisdom, they seek God. Maybe you are that person!

I can remember first learning deep truths about Scripture around age thirteen. I prayed to the Lord saying, "I will know that You are real and powerful God, if you fix my family!" In my young, ignorant, selfish, and sinful mind, I had no idea the audacity I exhibited in demanding such a stipulation of God. I am embarrassed about it at times when I meet people who bowed before God with pure and unrestrained faith while I cynically insisted He must prove Himself to me. God, however, knows our hearts better than we do and can often see what we are really asking of Him even when we cannot.

God in His great mercy and grace did fix my family. I spent the next twenty-five years with a closer and more wonderful relationship with my earthly father than

I ever could have hoped for until the Lord took him home to heaven. I did not deserve having God demonstrate His power in my family in this way. God could have demanded my obedience and obeisance without providing it, but for some reason that only He knows, He indeed answered my foolish and selfish prayer. Maybe He saw in my childish heart how desperately I wanted to believe in Him but how afraid I was of being let down. He knew my heart needed healing, and He graciously bolstered my tenuous faith.

My grandparents modeled marvelous faith, and I wanted to believe with the same level of assurance and peace that they did. We know of others in our lives—maybe it is our own story too—of how we came to the cross because we sought help for a circumstance rather than our soul. We were looking for a quick fix, or maybe even posed a brazen demand for an answer from God before pledging Him our allegiance. Yes, it is God's desire for us to come to Him, to seek Him, and to know and believe Him, but here is a hard truth: He is the One who sets the terms.

Not everyone who comes to Him is really seeking Him, and the Righteous Judge knows the difference! The people of Ezekiel's day sought God for His blessings, not for a relationship with God Himself. God does not want to merely change your circumstances, dear one. He wants to change *you*. And while a change in circumstances does sometimes graciously occur, it is the change within our heart that He is after. This comes through seeking a relationship with Him. Through handing over your heart in surrender.

READ EZEKIEL 14:1–8.

Who was coming before Ezekiel and what were they doing?

How does God respond to them?

What was God's purpose in concealing Himself?

What does God insist the people must do?

Consider this explanation on the role of the prophets: "By the order of the prophets, the Lord enabled His people to walk into the unknown future with faith and obedience, trusting in the sovereign God, not, as the pagan, trying to secure and control the future by magic rites."[11] God saw straight into the exiles' hearts; they do not want an answer from God, they are seeking to secure His favorable blessing on them. We do the same thing when we "behave" for a while and then seek God for our requests.

When God says He will answer them "as he comes with the multitude of his idols" (v. 4), He is saying that just as people cannot seek truth from an idol, neither shall they be able to hear truth from God. Until they honor God as the only truth, God will not speak truth to them through His prophet Ezekiel. God would remain silent. We must remember that the people sought answers from false prophets and from fortune-tellers, yet now, when none of these empty promises came to pass, and they had exhausted all other resources, they decided to finally seek the Lord.

Many scholars believe that the exiles have been in captivity for over six years now. Yet how many times has Ezekiel spoken of the elders coming to inquire of him for direction from God? *Only twice.* Does that sound to you like a people desperate to hear from God?

God clearly lays out His terms: *If you want answers from Me, then you need to confess the futility of all the other sources of guidance you seek—and long for My answers alone. As long as My answers remain only one of many which you seek, I shall remain silent.* This may seem harsh and hard to grasp. Many times in our churches today, we hear that God is just waiting, pleading with us to allow Him the opportunity to reveal Himself to us, if we would only come ask Him. Please understand: God does want to reveal Himself! But He wants to reveal Himself as God, not a god, our last resort, a nice idea, or just another option. He wants to reveal Himself as LORD: the Most High, the Sovereign One, who holds our future and the future of the entire world within His hands.

God sees the hearts of His people. They are looking to God for answers, yet refusing to acknowledge Him as God in their hearts. God then goes on to speak to the false prophets themselves.

READ EZEKIEL 14:8–10.

What does God say He will do to the false prophets?

Owth. Kind of sounds like "ouch" doesn't it? *Owth* is the Hebrew word for "sign," meaning:

"Miraculous sign, proof . . . *owth* showed or confirmed anything in the past, present or future. It excited attention or consideration. It distinguished one thing from another. It was an inducement to believe what was affirmed, professed, or promised. *It was the acid test of prophecy.*"[12]

Destruction. That would be the sign. God would prove their falsehood by displaying His impending judgment leading to their destruction. Ouch indeed.

God also says something a bit confusing here, so I want to make sure we understand it fully. Fill in the blanks in Ezekiel 14:9:

And if the prophet is _____ and speaks a word, I, the LORD, _____that prophet, and I will stretch out my hand against him.

Does God ever deceive His people? How are we to understand this? God would allow these false prophets to continue to chase after their evil desires. He would allow them to continue in their deception. Maybe they did not want to face the truth of their own sinfulness and therefore could not confront others. Maybe they preferred the approval of man and did not want to tell the people something they did not want to hear. Maybe the acceptance of the people and the status it afforded them proved more important than the approval of God. We do not know exactly what motivated them to continue to prophesy things from their own hearts rather than the harsh warnings of God, but God would allow them to continue to preach peace and prosperity while impending destruction awaited them.

Paul explains this process of deception in Romans 1:18–21. Fill in these blanks for verse 21:

For although they knew God, they did not _____ as God or give thanks to him, but they became _____ _____.

When we fail to acknowledge God, and begin to view Him as only one of many options, our thinking becomes futile. We become deceived. And until we repent and return to the Lord acknowledging Him as God, we remain in our deception. We can see why God repeats His same purpose nearly fifty times in the book of

Ezekiel: *Then they will know that I am the LORD.* When we acknowledge God as the rightful Lord over all, the faithful, covenant-keeping God, our Lord, then deceptions shatter. God gave the people every opportunity to acknowledge Him as the only rightful deity, but they continued to drag along their idols. So God allowed them to remain in their deception.

How about us? Do we have someone in our lives who will warn us of consequences as well as God's promises? Someone who speaks truth to us even when we may not want to hear it? Who is it for you, and how well do you receive truth from them?

Consider three things:

1. You were meant to have that kind of relationship with others. It takes great commitment to have honesty and transparency in a relationship. A person who is willing to speak the truth into your life is someone who is willing to invest in your life. Do you have a relationship like this—of mutual respect and truth between yourself and someone else? Your spouse, or if not married, someone else close? We ought to as believers. Secrecy is synonymous with idolatry.

2. We also ought to have these types of relationships within our church family. Don't wait for someone else to come along and start investing in your life. Seek out someone in whom you can invest. Join a small group, serve in an area of ministry, or attend a Sunday school class. Begin to build relationships where bonds of trust become forged. Building healthy relationships in which we point others toward truth, reminding them of God's sovereignty and holiness, take time, energy, and trust. They are not built overnight.

3. Your pastor should be a person who preaches truth. He should use his position of leadership to challenge and push you to new levels of faith, commitment, and obedience. He is not meant to entertain you for an hour and fill you with warm fuzzies every Sunday. He needs to teach the truths of Scripture corporately over the church, and sometimes those truths might be a little, let's say, "ouchy." However, he probably does not have the capacity to speak truth into each member's individual circumstances, which is why we need other members of our church family who know the details of our lives more intimately to speak truth to us as well. We need other members of the church to encourage us to apply the truths of Scripture to our daily lives.

Know your why. Have you heard that phrase? God ends this prophecy giving the people clear understanding of the why.

READ EZEKIEL 14:10–11.

What three reasons does God give for destroying the false prophets among the exiles?

1.

2.

3.

By what name does God declare Himself at the end of verse 11?

Look carefully at these two definitions with my emphasis added:

LORD: Master, i.e., a title of the true God with *a focus on the authority and majesty of a ruler.*[13]

Yahweh: Jehovah, the Lord as a euphemism for *Adonai* in most versions, the name of the one true God, *with a focus on sure existence and His relationship to His covenant persons and peoples.*[14]

God wants us to focus on Him as the one with the authority to rule, yet also with certainty of relationship. The exiles of Ezekiel's day focused on the latter while neglecting the former. They wanted their way and for God to bless it. They wanted to go home and have everything return to the old ways. But God insisted on doing a new thing. And until they allowed God to rule they would forever misunderstand the relationship He longed to have with them.

When we seek God for answers, we must be prepared to hear and obey them, even when they are not what we had hoped to hear. Even when they are a bit "ouchy." He alone holds our future in His hands. And His ways are often beyond us. Dear one, do you seek an answer from God? Or do you seek God Himself? There is a difference . . . maybe the difference between returning to the old ways or inviting revival.

THE FINAL THREE

EZEKIEL 14:12–23

Americans hold an intense fascination for reality television shows with contests. We have contests for dancing and for singing; we have bake-offs; we have match-ups for home decorating, business ventures, races of all types; and then there are those most extreme competitions of who can survive the longest in death-defying climatic conditions in some remote location. I think it is our constant default to compare and discern how we rank in this world that fosters this fascination. Each question is designed to answer one final question: Who is the best at _____? That is the American way, after all, to be the best at something. We are not significant unless we are the best. I heard a dad once say to his eight-year-old, "Son, you know what second place is, right?" Annoyed, but trying to feign his dad's enthusiasm to give it all he had to win the game, the little boy muttered, "Yep, first loser."

Well, in today's portion of Scripture, God lays out His own reality contest, His top three.

READ EZEKIEL 14:12–14.

Who are the final three God mentions?

Who could these men save in the wake of God's judgment?

Look back at Genesis 6:5–9. How does God describe mankind in these verses?

Yet, who found favor in the eyes of the Lord?

According to Genesis 7:1, who entered the ark with Noah?

God does not tell us that Noah's family was righteous. He tells us that Noah was righteous. Nevertheless, all of Noah's family was saved in the ark. Let's move on to our next contestant.

READ DANIEL 2:1–24.

Who did Nebuchadnezzar order to be killed and why?

How did Daniel act as intercessor, and who was spared?

Daniel's great faith saved some skin beyond his own. Now let's look at contestant number three.

READ JOB 42:7–9.

Who was the Lord angry with, and why?

How were they saved from their folly?

Now, let's see what these righteous men have to do with the Lord's prophecies through Ezekiel.

READ EZEKIEL 14:12–23.

Who would these final three be able to save in Jerusalem according to the Lord?

How does God describe the destruction of Jerusalem?

How would the exiles feel when they witnessed the conduct and the actions of those who fled the Holy City?

Why would they feel that way?

My Bible teacher in high school used to say, "God has no grandchildren." We must each make our own decision to follow Christ. No one makes it for us and just because we may have a Christian heritage, that does not make us a Christian. Just because the people lived in Jerusalem did not mean they had the Lord's favor. We must all be accountable before the Lord individually, not because of location or lineage. Being raised in a Christian home where generations of Christians have lived does not make me a Christian any more than parking myself on the floor of my garage makes me a car.

These three righteous men enabled others to be spared. But the depravity among the people of Israel had become so pronounced that even if a few righteous remained within its walls, God's judgment would not be thwarted. The destruction of Jerusalem remained imminent. The exiles held on to the hope that if enough righteous remained, God would spare their beloved city. God emphatically declared otherwise.

The Lord wanted the exiles to understand the need for such judgment on the people. He desired for them to stop straying from the Lord and turning to idols. We have a hard time comprehending their attachment to Jerusalem because our center of worship is so different today. For them, the city of Jerusalem and the temple held the presence of God. Not only was it their center of worship, it contained the means to maintain their relationship with God through sacrifices on the altar. God had made it clear that sacrifices were never to be made on any other altar than the one in Jerusalem. And it was through the sacrifice that they maintained God's favor. To be unable to worship in such a way brought spiritual devastation and God's departure. God's point? *If you are not intent on worshiping Me in the prescribed manner, you shall no longer be able to worship Me at all.*

It is hard for us to imagine being stripped of all means of worship in our modern-day evangelical context. Unable to gather. Our Bibles confiscated. No livestreamed sermons or biblical teaching. No crosses anywhere in sight. This seems unthinkable to us, but for the exiles who had been kept from their temple festivals and sacrifices for six long years, their deepest desire was to return to the Holy City of Jerusalem and be in God's presence once again. Yet, they still seemed to misunderstand how far their hearts remained from God. In many ways their physical distance from the holy city of Jerusalem depicted the spiritual distance of their hearts from the intimacy God desired to have with them.

We must ask ourselves an important question: On what are we basing our security—our religious heritage? Our government? Our security does not exist in a building, a law, a government, or a nation. Our security rests in God alone and His righteous judgments. On Christ's death and resurrection and our promise of His return. Of eternal life in heaven. This is our hope and security. This and this alone. The final three could not save Israel. Only Jesus saves today. Is your hope in Him alone?

THE PURPOSE OF REVIVAL

Our Beautiful Purpose

VESSELS AND VINES

EZEKIEL 15

My dad loved to garden. We never grew grapes but we did grow tomatoes, watermelon, and pumpkins, all of which grow on vines. Unlike a tree, which specifically grows upward, the branches of a vine, called canes, need to be directed so the blossoms and fruit have plenty of space to catch enough sunlight. And after you harvest, you need to prune the branches way back so the plant doesn't get all tangled up within itself and leave no room for future blossoms. If there are too many branches on the vine, there won't be enough nutrients to maintain adequate blooms. The vinedresser in a vineyard must prune dead branches every year or the vine will wither, and no fruit will be produced.

The vine supplies all of the nutrients to the branches. However, if too many dead or dying branches receive part of the nutrients, the thriving branches will begin to wither because there are no longer enough nutrients for all of them. These branches or canes must be pruned back so that adequate life can be supplied to the strongest canes.

Unlike a solid tree trunk, the wood of a vine is pliable, allowing it to be steered and secured to stakes and trellises and trimmed annually. No one cuts off the branches of a vine to build structures, as the wood is too soft. The only useful thing to be done with pruned pieces of a vine is burning them as firewood.

God offers a searing rebuke regarding His people in Ezekiel 15. They are a "useless vine" and "good only for fire." He also prophesies as to their fate within the city of Jerusalem. They will be burned.

READ EZEKIEL 15:1–8.

What specifically did God say would happen to the city of Jerusalem and its inhabitants?

What would the people know as a result?

For what reason had God decided on this course of action?

In light of the vine analogy, what "nutrients" do you think God intended for His people to bring to the world?

Jesus also referred to Himself as a vine and His Father as the vinedresser. Read through John 15:1–17. How many times does Jesus use the word "abide" in this passage? (Some translations use the word "remain.")

According to Jesus' description, of what use would a branch be that did not abide within, or remain on, the vine?

What will a branch inevitably do if it remains on a vine that the vinedresser has effectively cared for?

What two things occur when we bear much fruit?

According to John 15:10, what must we do to abide in Jesus' love? And what commandment does He specifically give us in verse 12?

Jesus repeats this commandment in John 15:17. Write it here:

Based on these verses—John 15:10, 12, and 17—what might be some examples of a "fruitful" life?

If Jesus were trying to decide if a particular church family was bearing much fruit, what evidence do you suppose He would seek?

Let's go back to the vine analogy. Our pumpkin vines only grew pumpkins, just like we only found tomatoes on our tomato trellis. The vine only produces one type of fruit, not multiple types of fruit. Based on Jesus' emphasis in John 15, what specific fruit does Jesus want to see His disciples bearing?

Let's spend some time today abiding in the Vine. Toward the back of this study book you will find two large hearts. In the first heart, write a list of names of the people you love most dearly in this world. To love *them* is to obey *Him*. But we will be unable to love well and unselfishly in our own power; we need to be securely attached to the vine, allowing His life to flow into us. Pause and ask Jesus how to love each of those people well today.

In the heart on the opposite page, ask Jesus who is on His heart for you to love. It may be someone hard for you to imagine offering love toward. Offer yourself to Jesus as His vessel to flow into and bear fruit by your willingness to offer His love to them. Ask Him for practical ways to show love to even the most unlovable. Jesus promised that when we ask for Him to love others through us, He will give us the ability (see John 15:16).

Pruning away opinions and perceptions. Strengthening from the True Vine. Jesus pouring life through us as His vessel. This is how we become full of joy. This is revival.

STRAIGHT TO THE HEART

EZEKIEL 16:1–43

I can picture April 28, 2004, on my calendar. That little square had a giant red heart on it. That was the day Eliana would be born and we would finally get to meet her. My mom and I bought no less than ten outfits trying to decide what she would wear home from the hospital. The car seat had been securely fastened into the back seat weeks before her arrival, along with a packed diaper bag, as we meticulously prepared for the big day. Jonathan and I had waited over ten years for this moment, and we could hardly contain ourselves over the excitement of it all. Our firstborn child's arrival.

God sharply contrasted Israel's birth to our sentiments over Eliana's arrival.

READ EZEKIEL 16:1–7.

The reference to the Canaanites means the Israelites had acted like the spiritual offspring of pagans. Why was the newborn, "Jerusalem," spoken of as abandoned?

See verses 6–7. What did God say to Israel as He found her?

The Hebrew word in verse 7 is *hayah* and means to come to life, flourish, revive, restore to life and nurture.[15] God paints a tender and intimate word picture, puncturing the heart of His people. A parent nurturing an infant daughter. His care so constant, she would grow to be a beautiful young woman.

READ EZEKIEL 16:8–14. Here God uses another tender and intimate word picture: the wedding night and the joining of a bride to her husband.

Describe below how God cared for His beautiful bride:

God intends these descriptions to pierce through the heart of His people. God desired that the reminder of His tender care for them would move them to repentance. To cause them to revel in His kindness and to return to relationship with Him as Israel's father and husband. But sadly, they spurned His affection.

READ EZEKIEL 16:15–34.

What did Israel do with the garments God had given her?

What did she do with her gold?

What did she do with her oil, flour, and honey?

What did she do with her children?

What did the nation of Israel fail to remember?

With what four nations did God tell Israel she had "played the whore"?

According to verse 30, where did Israel's sickness reside?

How was Israel even more lewd than a prostitute?

We cannot remove this reproach of God from the relationship Israel held with God. Imagine a father confronting his daughter over her prostitution. She took the clothing he had bought her, the food he had given her, and the golden ring of purity he placed on her, and she ran away and gave it to a pimp on the corner. Imagine a husband coming home to find the remains of a candlelit dinner on his dining room table and a strange man in his bedroom with his arms wrapped around his wife. God intends this language to be jolting. He goes to great lengths to jar His people out of complacency. His heart is broken. His anger incited. His judgment severe.

According to Ezekiel 16:35–43, what type of judgment would God bring on His rebellious daughter/unfaithful wife?

Since we don't form gold statues and burn incense in front of them, nor burn our children on pyres, it would be easy to conclude these stern warnings of God do not apply to us. But by examining these practices in greater context we can easily gather our own applications.

There is nothing symbolic about the objects the ancient Israelites used to engage in idolatry. God is talking about their actual clothing, jewelry, and possessions. They offered these luxuries to foreign gods in order to secure their favor.

With Eliana being born on April 28, Mother's Day arrived only a few days afterward. What a celebration on that first Mother's Day! For countless Mother's Days I had sobbed buckets wondering if I would ever become a mother. And now through the selfless act of a brave birth mother, I held a beautiful baby girl in my arms. In order to remember this wonderful moment, my husband surprised me with an exquisite silver bracelet from Tiffany's. It was an extravagant gift, and he wanted me to always have it in remembrance of the marvelous joy that we felt on that first Mother's Day when God had graciously given us our precious baby girl. He didn't intend it to be a symbol of status. He simply felt that God had blessed us with such an extravagant gift in Eliana, he wanted to commemorate the gift we had been given with something truly beautiful.

A couple of weeks later, Dale, a missionary to Thailand, had been invited to speak to our church. He told how he would pose as a man who housed a prostitution site for little girls, who were sometimes as young as six or seven, and buy them off the auction block. He would redeem them from the life of slavery they had been headed to and then take them to an orphanage, where they would be raised by loving Christian missionaries. They would learn about Christ and they would be taught a trade so they could support themselves once grown. After all these years, I still remember Dale mentioning the price he would pay for each little girl and thinking: "He could have saved two little girls for the price of this bracelet on my wrist." He could have saved another for the price of my handbag that carries my keys and my lipstick. Another for the price of my shoes that I only wore on Sundays to church. And another for my winter coat.

As I sat adorned in luxury, I suddenly felt sick. I hadn't known the plight of the little girls Dale was bringing before us that morning when I had purchased these items, but what if I *had* been aware of it? Would I have chosen not to purchase these accessories and given Dale the money to redeem a child's life? I liked to think, Absolutely! but I wasn't so sure. I am convinced that one of the reasons we sometimes don't like to have missionaries speak in our churches is that they force us to ask ourselves these tough questions.

We would rather continue to adorn ourselves with beauty than sacrifice ourselves. We carefully put on our costly garments and gold and silver to show the world how important we are. But God told us in Ezekiel 16:7 that we are important because we are His. When we take our garments and use them to form an identity or to claim importance with them, they have become idols to us.

What are some ways that we can take our clothing, our jewelry, and our wardrobe accessories and use them to engage in idolatry?

I'm not saying we ought to run around in tunics of burlap to please God. We see God adorning His bride in beautiful clothing to honor her. God purposefully reared infant Israel, made a covenant with her, and made her beautiful. God does not condemn us for delighting in beauty. Wearing a special silver bracelet to remember God's faithfulness and kindness in my life does not make me an idolater. It was God who blessed Israel with her abundance. But when we adorn ourselves in pursuit of significance or satisfaction, we begin to slide down a slippery slope. God did not rebuke Israel for her bounty and love of beauty. His anger was aroused because she had forgotten the purpose of her beauty. God adorned her to show the world His sovereignty and benevolence, His kindness and care: all aspects of His character that stood in sharp contrast to the foreign gods the pagan nations foolishly strove to appease. But instead of using their beauty as a tool to teach the surrounding nations about their God, Israel became prideful and flaunted her wealth.

What are some practical ways we can demonstrate to the world these
characteristics of God?

Look carefully at the progression of events. In 16:13–14, Israel radiated beauty
and she belonged solely to the Lord. But in verse 15, we see her begin to flaunt
her beauty and grow prideful because of it. They no longer saw the necessity of
belonging to the Lord alone and they began to flirt with idolatry. By verse 16,
they have embraced idolatry fully and they are actively worshiping the gods of
the pagan nations around them. Interestingly, pagan nations worshiped idols of
fertility and prosperity, and Israel already had so much compared to them. The
time of David's and Solomon's reigns are sometimes referred to as the Golden Age
of Israel. Solomon's wealth was known worldwide at this time, and the temple he
constructed was exquisite. God is speaking of Israel's past splendor and how they
had responded to God's blessings. God had showered upon Israel great wealth, but
there arose in her a pride and discontent from which she had to make sure she was
not missing out on anything in worshiping the Lord alone.

We have the same foolishness when we allow the shiny things of this world
to bring us into temptation because we are afraid we might be missing out on
something the world has to offer.

What are some of the things the world offers that tempt you the most?

We can be tempted by riches, power, fame, success, acceptance from others, by pleasure, food—the list is endless. But we have already been given so much more than the world could ever offer. We must trust in the perfectness of God's provision and His promise of perfection in the fullness of time. What more could we want? Anything the world has to offer is merely a false substitute. Here is the root of the matter and a hard truth: When we are tempted by the things of the world, it is an indicator that we don't really believe that God is enough. We buy into the lie that He is holding out on us. We believe there are parts of the world that are actually able to bring us greater happiness than God Himself. If we forego those earthly pleasures, God will not really be enough to satisfy our deepest longings. You might want to look up Chris Tomlin's song "Enough," in which he beautifully expresses this truth.

Do you really believe that He is enough to satisfy you? Would the loss of His presence in your life pierce your heart, or would you shrug in indifference? Spend a few moments thinking through a typical day in your life. How consistently do you live in awareness of the Father's presence with you? Share your heart with your Father below . . .

LIKE MOTHER, LIKE DAUGHTER

EZEKIEL 16:44–63

Think back to the last wedding you attended. Picture the bride in your mind. How long do you imagine she took to prepare herself for her groom? My favorite moment at any wedding is when the bride and the groom first lock eyes on each other. It's as if everyone in the room fades and they focus solely on each other. From that moment forward it's as though they cannot take their eyes off of one another.

Can you imagine a bride walking down the aisle in a dirty dress or a lewd garment? With overly painted face and disheveled hair? How about a bride who begins to flirt with every man she passes down the aisle because she knows she has spent hours preparing herself and she is now perfect in beauty (Ezek. 16:14)? Have you ever seen anything like that in any wedding you have attended? I doubt it. A bride does not simply wish to be beautiful, she wishes to be beautiful in the eyes of her groom.

Here is a tougher question: Do we as the bride of Christ have that same longing and desire to be beautiful for Him? Just as the bride walking down the aisle is unable to take her eyes off her groom waiting for her at the altar, do we have our eyes so fixed on Jesus waiting for us to be united with Him that we would not even take a glimpse at any other potential groom?

Read 2 Corinthians 11:2–3. What was Paul's fear for the church at Corinth?

The bride in today's passage, the nation of Israel, sought the love of others beyond her husband. God walks through her lineage and reviews how she exceeded the lewdness of her mother and sisters.

READ EZEKIEL 16:44–52.

What sins did Israel's mother and sisters commit?

Fill in the blanks: Your mother was a _____ and your father an _____. And your elder sister is _____ . . . and your younger sister is _____.

According to God, which of the five family members was the most unrighteous?

List the five things of which Sodom was guilty of according to verses 49–50:

1.

2.

3.

4.

5.

Israel's haughtiness disgraced God. In this prophecy, He takes them all the way back to the days of Noah, a man righteous before God. Noah had three sons: Shem, Ham, and Japheth. Israel was a descendant of Shem. That is why sometimes the Jewish people are referred to as Semites. The term is a derivative of Shem. Ham gave birth to Canaan. Both the Hittites and the Amorites were descendants of Canaan. Essentially, they are cousins and of the same lineage, so Israel lacks reasons for her boasting.

The sisters demonstrated even more reasons for Israel to swallow her pride. Samaria had been conquered by Assyria nearly 150 years prior to the southern tribes of Israel. They intermarried with their captors and established their own system of worship outside of Jerusalem: two things strictly forbidden by God. As a result, the southern tribes surrounding Jerusalem spurned them for lack of racial purity and religious practice.

Sodom epitomized the place of sinfulness in the mind of the Israelites. God destroyed the city with fire after rescuing Abraham's nephew Lot. It's where the word "sodomy" originated, meaning sexual acts among members of the same sex or humans engaging in sexual acts with animals.[16]

Now this is where it gets interesting. If Ezekiel were to have gone around and taken a poll of his fellow exiles and asked them what they thought the sins of Sodom had been, I imagine they would have said the same thing: sodomy. I'm also pretty sure they would not have cited excess of food, or gluttony, or apathy. What was God getting at here?

I think He is raising the point that it was easy to judge the city of Sodom for her apparent, outward sins, but the sins of the heart—arrogance, haughtiness, apathy, and selfishness—these are much harder to identify, *yet are just as heinous* to the heart of God. I think the modern church can also agree on a handful of identifiable sins, but the question we should be asking ourselves is how we handle the sins God mentions in regard to Sodom: pride in our riches and our ease, and apathy toward those less fortunate. All inward sins of the heart.

Jesus also taught about these inward sins of the heart.

Read Luke 18:9–14. According to this story, who was the more righteous?

Read Psalm 82:3–4. What does God command regarding the poor?

Read Proverbs 14:31. How does our treatment of the poor demonstrate our attitude toward God?

God in His great grace does not leave us in our depravity and destruction. He promises deliverance.

READ EZEKIEL 16:53–63.

What does God promise to do for Samaria, Sodom, and Israel?

What would God remember, and what would it cause Him to do as a result?

What would Israel know and what would she remember?

Who would atone for Israel?

We see this promise played out in living color before us in John 4:1–30: Jesus the Messiah sent to atone for our sins. To whom did Jesus first reveal Himself as the Messiah, resulting in the first messianic revival?

It is God's truth and faithfulness toward us that always reveals the truth about ourselves! Over five hundred years after Ezekiel, God works not through the outwardly righteous but through the repentant heart—a train wreck of a woman from the wrong side of the tracks. A Samaritan living in sin. God does not change His mind about keeping His promises to us because of our own unfaithfulness. No, He keeps His covenant based on His faithfulness alone. There is nothing we can do or not do to cause God to act unfaithfully.

God said the nation of Israel would be rendered silent when they remembered their wickedness. This implies two things: they have no defense against their behavior nor any room for judgment upon another for theirs. They would realize that their righteousness came from the Lord alone and that He alone was the judge of sin and worthiness. They would not dare to condemn another.

Just like the nation of Israel, we cannot pigeonhole sin into only those acts most obvious. We must also examine the inward sins of the heart. Arrogance, self-righteousness, overindulgence in the luxuries of this world, and lack of concern for the poor and needy are easy sins to commit in our culture. In fact, in many instances our culture even applauds them, commanding us to flaunt our success and step proudly onto our pedestals of accomplishments and possessions. We would be wise to kneel down and ask God to shed His glorious light on any hidden sins within the dark places of our heart.

THE EAGLE AND THE VINE

EZEKIEL 17

Most people are familiar with this old adage: The third time's the charm. I'm not sure where it originated, but it conveys the idea that even if the first and second attempt result in failure, generally by the third go around you will experience success.

Take a look closely at Ezekiel 15:1, 16:1, and now 17:1. Record the first eight words in each of these chapters below:

Ezekiel 17 encompasses the third time God will speak an allegory or parable to the exiles to explain His justification for His impending judgment on the city of Jerusalem. Unfortunately, not even the third time will be the charm in bringing the exiles into agreement with God regarding His plan and purposes. It will however, prepare them for what is ahead.

Read Ezekiel 17 in its entirety.

Let's work through this. An eagle comes to Lebanon, which stands for Israel here, and breaks off the topmost branch of a cedar, which represents the ruling educated class, and planted them in a land of traders, representing Babylon. God is recounting what occurred in 605 BC when Nebuchadnezzar first attacked Jerusalem, carried off King Jehoiakim, and deported many citizens of Judah to Babylon, one of whom was Daniel. (See 2 Kings 24:1–2; 2 Chronicles 36:5–7; Daniel1:1–7.) The eagle represents King Nebuchadnezzar of Babylon.

Even though Judah had been taken captive by Nebuchadnezzar and the Babylonians, the vine, Israel, still flourished. Its branches were now turned toward Babylon, their ruling country, yet the vine still functioned, as it was planted in fertile, well-watered soil. But this vine sought another eagle to provide water for it. Israel sought the help of Pharaoh, king of Egypt, the second eagle in the parable. King Zedekiah, the vassal king set in place over Judah by King Nebuchadnezzar, rebelled against him and sought the aid of Pharaoh to overthrow the Babylonians.

Take a look at 2 Chronicles 36:1–6. Who ruled over Judah prior to Nebuchadnezzar taking charge?

Well, that's interesting. Apparently, they preferred their previous captors rather than the current Babylonians.

What does God say will happen as a result of this rebellion? (See Ezekiel 17:9–10.)

What will happen to King Zedekiah? (See Ezekiel 17:19–21.)

Here is the most fascinating part! King Nebuchadnezzar first arrived in 605 BC. Zedekiah revolted against him in 588 BC. Let's take a closer look at what year it is right now when Ezekiel is announcing this prophecy to the captives.

Record the time given in Ezekiel 8:1.

Record the time given in Ezekiel 20:1.

Most scholars agree that the events recorded thus far in the book of Ezekiel happened chronologically, so the messages given to Ezekiel in chapters 8–20 all happened within the sixth and seventh year of his exile. If Ezekiel was taken captive to Babylon in 597 BC, then this allegory that he is telling the people was announced in approximately 590 BC.

Do you see the remarkable part? God is giving the exiles a prophecy that Zedekiah's revolt will occur within the next two years. God is informing the exiles that it was

His plan all along for the southern kingdom of Judah to be taken captive by the Babylonians and the plan included them flourishing as Nebuchadnezzar's vassal state. However, King Zedekiah, whom Nebuchadnezzar had just appointed as his vassal, would choose to rebel against God's plan, therefore bringing death upon himself and destruction over the city of Jerusalem. For a third time, God informed the exiles that the judgment of Jerusalem was imminent, brought about by their own rebellion.

Read Jeremiah 27:12–15. What warning did God issue to Zedekiah before he chose to revolt against Nebuchadnezzar?

Read Daniel 4:28–33. What may have been Nebuchadnezzar's mental state leading Zedekiah to pursue his revolt against him?

The captives only know what is happening in Babylon. The remaining Jews only know what is happening within Judah. Daniel only knows what is transpiring in Nebuchadnezzar's court. But God sees the whole picture. He is working out His will and His ways everywhere at all times. In our limited view it may feel like God is far away or He has forgotten our plight. But God's Word shows us we are always within His sight and held by the grip of His grace. Part of being ready for revival involves believing God is doing His work beyond our limited scope of sight and our personal circumstances.

God had released Judah from her captivity to the Egyptians, making them subject to the Babylonians. He had in mind for them to flourish and provided them what they needed to do so, but they did not like God's plan. So they rebelled against God's plan, preferring to go back to their previous captors. We do not like to admit this, but we can do the same thing. God puts us in a circumstance, gives us the grace we need to flourish in it, but rather than accept our less than idyllic circumstances, we rebel against Him and seek the aid of others or rely on ourselves to change our current state. Then when we bring judgment on ourselves due to our rebellion, we blame God for all of it.

God is sovereign over all. There is not anyone or anything in your life of which He is not in control. When we fully believe and accept this, we stop seeking alliances with false saviors trying to regain a sense of control. Any other help is just another captor. We also stop insisting our limited circumstances must make sense to us, forgetting God is at work all over the world in ways we cannot see. Instead our lives become marked with His gracious ability to bear fruit no matter the circumstance.

Please hear my heart in this. I know there are some of you who have suffered inexplicable tragedy and hurt in this life. I am in no way trying to offer a simple platitude or discount the pain and agony you have suffered or are currently suffering. I am fully aware that healing and grieving are long, arduous processes and involve a journey unique to each person and circumstance. My desire is not to seem apathetic to anyone's pain; my heart is to encourage you to believe that God is able to carry you through it even when you cannot find your way or you feel so broken you cannot move. God alone is the perfect Healer who knows when you need to just be held and heard and when you need to be nudged and taught.

Is there a circumstance in your life you label as less than ideal or even difficult? If so, can you acquiesce in God's ability to accomplish something through it, though it may remain beyond your understanding until you reach heaven?

Only our God can cause us to flourish in difficult circumstances. And only our God can cause us to be fruitful when we feel stripped away from where we belong. Our God can bring fruitfulness out of even the most horrific of circumstances. It is His desire for us to be fruitful, and it is also His desire for us to be *willing* to bear fruit wherever He may plant us. He can cause us to bear fruit no matter how dry and withered we may feel. You've seen the saying "Bloom where you're planted." Are you willing to bloom where God has planted you, or do you wish He would uproot you and move you to another place or circumstance? Are you willing to bear fruit for Him now, or are you like the people of Judah, insisting He replant them where they wanted and felt they deserved to be?

Think for a moment about your difficult circumstance you identified above. How could God use that circumstance to bear fruit in your life and allow you to show the world what He is like?

Before you close your study book, write out a prayer of surrender for God to help you bloom wherever He has planted you today. Maybe it starts with just handing over your hurt and your emotions to Him and the moving forward comes later. The first step is acknowledging that He knows your pain, cares about your hurt, and is able to bring fruitfulness to your life in spite of it all.

WEEK 4 | DAY 5

SOUR GRAPES

EZEKIEL 18

What is the primary complaint my teenagers toss at me? "But Mom, that's not fair!" Anyone else hear that from their children? And what's my number one answer? "Life's not fair!" We can all think of things in life that are not fair. The world is full of injustice in every corner. What is justice anyway? How would you define it? Some would claim it involves giving everyone the exact same thing. Others suggest it is not giving everyone the same exact thing, rather it would be giving each person exactly what they need, which could be different for each of us. That's the problem with justice, we usually cannot agree on what is fair in the first place!

If I presented a scenario to ten adults and asked them what would be a fair outcome, I would most likely get ten different answers. So, rather than asking, "What is fair?" maybe the better question would be, "Who should decide what is fair?"

In Ezekiel 18, the nation of Israel accused God of being unfair. The amazing thing in this passage of Scripture is that God actually takes the time to defend Himself! When my children complain to me about unfairness, I rarely make the effort to explain my decision. Mostly because I know they are merely complaining for the sake of complaining, not because they wish to truly have a productive debate on how to best arrive at justice.

To think that our almighty, holy, heavenly Father would take the time to explain Himself to His whiny children—which describes each of us at times—makes me incredulous over His kindness and patience. Who are we to even demand an answer? How great is the love of our Father!

In Ezekiel 15–17, God laid out three parables or allegories to describe the history of the nation of Israel and how they had turned away from God. He laid out His faithfulness and kindness to them and reminded them that He had raised them up for the purpose of being a light to the nations and to show the world the greatness and goodness of Israel's God. What did God hope within His heart? That the people might repent and turn back to Him. Ezekiel 18 gives us a picture of what they chose to do instead. Rather than taking personal responsibility for their waywardness, they blamed their ancestors for their sinfulness and claimed they were being punished due to their predecessor's poor choices.

Read Jeremiah 31:29–30. What were the people inside the walls of Jerusalem saying and what was God telling them?

READ EZEKIEL 18:1–9.

The people eating sour grapes represented a euphemism claiming that the punishment Judah currently faced came about due to the sins of their ancestors. In other words, they were being unfairly punished for the sins of their forefathers. Whom does God insist is actually responsible for their sin?

Look carefully at Ezekiel 18:5–9. Put a check mark beside all of the descriptions of a righteous man.

Does not worship idols on the mountain shrines

Honors women

Does not oppress anyone

Returns what he borrows

Does not take anything that does not belong to him

Is generous to the hungry and needy

Pursues justice

Follows God's laws

Acts faithfully in all his ways

Put a star next to the description that is easiest for you. Put a heart next to the description most difficult. Ask God to give you a heart like His to be able to love others in the way that He does.

According to God, who gets to decide what is fair? God does. He says, "The soul who sins shall die" (v. 4). God insists that the judgment soon to befall His people is a result of their personal sin, not the sins of someone else. The question we now must ask ourselves is: Who are we blaming for our sinful behavior? Who in your family ate sour grapes? According to God, that does not give us an excuse for our sin. What are some of the sour sayings you may have heard while you were growing up? Perhaps:

I come from a family of yellers.

My parents used to comfort me with food.

My mom used to keep things from my dad just to keep the peace.

What happens in this house stays in this house.

You'd better stop that crying before I give you something to cry about!

You ought to be ashamed of yourself! What shame you will bring upon this family!

You will never amount to a hill of beans!

And somehow, we find ourselves repeating those same patterns. But what hope do we find in Romans 6:1–11?

READ EZEKIEL 18:10–20.

Does God blame a righteous man for having a wicked son? Who is to blame, according to God?

I want to pause here for a moment. Our tendency in Christian circles when we see wayward or prodigal children is to try to discover the "why" behind the waywardness. We want to ensure that our own children or grandchildren do not suffer from the same rebellious state. We want to find some sort of parental error or downfall to judge. According to God, the most righteous of men can have a wayward son. If you have a prodigal, you must stop beating yourself up over it. The enemy may be using guilt to plague you unnecessarily and to hinder you from effectively ministering to your wayward child or elsewhere as he piles upon you his shaming lies. If God does not give up on His wayward children, then neither shall we.

Let's read on. I found this next portion of Scripture so encouraging!

According to Ezekiel 18:21–29, what hope do we have for a prodigal?

Your wayward child still has room for repentance. Furthermore, their offspring can turn and choose to follow the Lord also. I have heard lots of different teachings on generational sin. I am by no means a theologian, but in piecing together portions of Scripture there is something I have noticed.

According to 1 John 1:9–10, how are we forgiven and cleansed from sin?

I think one reason why generational sin remains is because we often cease to acknowledge some of these long-held patterns in our lives as sin. We succumb to them with attitudes like, "That's just the way my dad is." Or "My mom has always been quick-tempered." "That's how my brothers and I always solved arguments." It's so familiar and habitual to us we have never taken the time to hold the behaviors and attitudes up to the light of God's Law. And never acknowledged nor confessed them as sin, nor asked forgiveness for so readily adopting them into our own thought life and behavioral patterns. Instead we cite the sinful patterns of our family members as a convenient excuse to keep on sinning ourselves.

Remember on day one of our homework this week the care the vinedresser must give to the vineyard in order for the grapevine to flourish and the grapes to be produced? It took intentionality and timeliness, right? Have you ever met someone who grew up in such a rotten vineyard full of brambles and overgrown vines that sorting it all out seemed daunting? Maybe that describes your family history. It would be easy to offer excuses like, "My family vineyard is such a disaster it would be utterly impossible to restore it and make it fruitful again! There are so many wild grapevines throughout, it would prove impossible for me to uproot them all, dig them all out, and bring restoration to it." Since the labor involved proves so exhausting, everyone ought to easily understand why they don't even bother trying.

Another person may suggest, "I've never even witnessed a well-cared-for vineyard. I don't even know what that looks like. How could someone expect me to be an adequate vinedresser?" They ought to be given a pass from even attempting to restore the vineyard. It would be unfair to even expect them to try. This was the attitude of Israel. They were all products of a rotten vineyard and should not have to do the hard work of restoring and reviving what their ancestors had allowed to devolve into utter unfruitfulness.

READ EZEKIEL 18:30–32.

How will God judge each person?

What does God long to give us?

God takes no pleasure in the death of anyone; rather He implores us to do what?

God did not desire to punish them. He longed to restore them. To dig up the wild weeds and thorn bushes and revive them from their withered state. God would do the work. They just needed to repent and return to Him. He would give them new hearts and new spirits who longed to pursue righteousness and fruitfulness. It was time to stop looking back. God invited them to look ahead at the life He had planned for them. Listen to God's plea: "Why will you die, O house of Israel?" Our God invites us to repent, return to Him and live!

What remains from your past that you can invite God to come and uproot today?

What sins of your ancestors have set your teeth on edge? It's time to acknowledge the ruin they have brought to your life!

Let's close today with the prayer of David:

> *Search me, O God, and know my heart! Try me and know my thoughts!*
> *And see if there be any grievous way in me, and lead me in the way everlasting!*
> PSALM 139:23–24

THE PATHWAY TO REVIVAL

Looking In, Bending Down, and Reaching Out

THE KING OF THE JUNGLE

EZEKIEL 19

Around the time Jonathan and I were leading a small group for newly married couples, personality tests to discover how you interacted with your spouse and responded to certain scenarios were popular. There were color tests, animal tests, acronyms, and all sorts of ways to help you discover your spouse's communication and emotional patterns as well as your own. The purpose? To help you understand each other more fully so your marriage would last "until death do us part." For the animal test, I scored highest as a lion, and it wasn't because I had big hair. I liked to take charge, be heard, and keep things in order. I'll leave it to your imagination how that fared during our first few years of marriage. God also describes the nation of Israel using the symbolism of a lion, and we are going to start with the end in mind. And as we read these prophecies given to us by Ezekiel, we cannot dismiss the personality, preferences, and emotional patterns of the prophet who delivered them. He did not receive these messages robotically, devoid of feeling or without emotional reactions to them.

READ EZEKIEL 19:1.

What is this oracle of Ezekiel to be regarded as and for whom?

Lamentation for Princes of Israel

Since it is highly unlikely anyone has FaceTimed you recently to offer up a lamentation, let me explain that a bit. "A 'lament' was a funeral song usually recited in honor of a dead person. The song generally stressed the good qualities of the departed and the tragedy or loss engendered by his death."[17] We cannot forget that while Ezekiel functions as God's spokesperson or prophet, he is also a human being who undoubtedly loved his homeland, took great pride in the exquisite temple in Jerusalem, and honored his heritage. To sing a song of the death of Israel's princes would most likely have been heartbreaking for Ezekiel. It means his homeland will be ravaged and the beautiful city of Jerusalem destroyed.

READ EZEKIEL 19:1–9.

These verses describe Israel's cubs. What happened to the first cub in verses 3–5?

*Devoured men
captured by Egypt*

What did the mother lioness, aka Israel, do as a result?

Brought out the spare

How is the next lion described in verses 6–7?

Like the prior but deadlier

laying waste to cities

What happened to this lion?

God continues to use allegories and parables to prophesy and explain His plan to
punish, purify, and ultimately restore Israel. Consider this God's personality test to
ensure that His relationship with His people does not remain only "until death do
us part," but for eternity. God recounts to the captives what has already occurred
within the land of Israel through this lament. God is recounting the history of
the previous three princes of Judah. King Josiah had been a righteous king before
God, but was killed in battle at Megiddo by Pharaoh Neco of Egypt. Afterward,
the people appointed Jehoahaz, Josiah's son, to become king in his father's place.
The first cub represents Jehoahaz. Pharaoh Neco came and captured him and
appointed Jehoiakim to be king in his place. In order to stay on the throne, he
paid heavy tribute to Pharaoh, taxing the people heavily and preying on them to
maintain his own power. (See 2 Kings 23:28–37.)

Although Pharaoh leaves him on the throne, Jehoiakim must contend with
another opposing power: the Babylonians. Nebuchadnezzar has now come
and made Jehoiakim his servant. But Jehoiakim rebelled against him, so
Nebuchadnezzar brought him to Babylon as a prisoner. Now his son Jehoiachin
becomes king, just for three months, and Nebuchadnezzar besieges Jerusalem
and carries away Jehoiachin along with several thousand captives. Most likely
the second cub is Jehoiachin. (Jehoiakim is skipped as a king in Ezekiel's oracle
because he had been appointed king by Pharaoh Neco and therefore never
recognized as a legitimate king by the people of Israel.) And after Jehoiachin is
taken to Babylon, Zedekiah, Jehoiachin's uncle, is appointed by Nebuchadnezzar
to become Judah's next king. (See 2 Kings 24:1–17.)

We are now in real time at this section of the lamentation. Zedekiah is currently
king. God points out to Ezekiel and his fellow captives that though Judah is as
strong as a lion, she shall be captured by the snare of the Babylonians.

READ EZEKIEL 19:10–14.

What metaphor does God use to describe Israel in these verses?

Vine in a vineyard

What happens to the vine?

Plucked and withered

Read 2 Kings 24:18–20. What foolish thing will King Zedekiah do?

Rebelled against Babylon

Read 2 Kings 25:1–12. What happened as a result?

Siege on Jerusalem
Took many captives

Nebuchadnezzar's army represents the "east wind" in Ezekiel's lamentation. He is prophesying the end of the dynasty of the kings of Judah. Hence the lamentation. No more princes of Judah exist. The people of Israel are a people "planted in the wilderness" of exile among the Babylonians.

Zedekiah was the last of Judah's kings to sit on the throne. Not until Christ comes to reign will a king from the land of Judah arise. The lament speaks of the death of Judah's kings until the King of kings returns. One of the hardest truths about revival is that it often requires a death of some sort before new life can start. For the nation of Israel, it required the destruction of their temple and their land. What areas of our lives need to die in order to revive us?

Take a few moments and prayerfully jot down some thoughts below:

HISTORY LESSONS

EZEKIEL 20

We studied Israel's proverb of the fathers eating sour grapes and the children's teeth being set on edge. A couple of contemporary proverbs are: "Hindsight is always 20/20" and "History is often our greatest teacher." After the last six chapters of Ezekiel pronouncing God's impending judgment on the people through dramatic word pictures in an effort to grip their hearts, God is now going to shift to a different approach: a direct history lesson.

You may have picked up on the fact that I can tend to be a bit wordy at times! Occasionally my husband will say to me, "Honey, I don't need the whole story, just give me the bullet points." Sometimes to get to the heart of what we want people to hear, less is more. This is what God is going to do now. Rather than emotional word pictures, God now moves to simple facts, bullet points of Israel's history.

- Who God is,

- What He has done for His people, and

- How they have responded along the way.

Ezekiel opens this chapter by telling us at exactly what point in Israel's history this encounter is taking place. It is the seventh year of Ezekiel's exile, so somewhere between 591 and 590 BC. Zedekiah is currently the king of Judah and has yet to revolt against Nebuchadnezzar as prophesied in the previous verses of Ezekiel 19.

It has been a little less than a year since the exiled elders have come to inquire of the Lord through Ezekiel. The last time they inquired of him was shortly after he had finished his demonstration of judgment against the land of Israel and Judah in Ezekiel 4 and 5. When they came at that time, Ezekiel was given the vision of idolatry in the temple, the idolaters killed, and the glory of the Lord departing from the temple (Ezek. 8–11). Ezekiel recounted this vision in dramatic detail for them. Since that last vision and this encounter, Ezekiel has demonstrated the imminent arrival of yet more exiles from Jerusalem and Judah (Ezek. 12), condemned the false prophets and idolaters (Ezek. 13–14), given the parable of the vine, the abandoned child who becomes the adulterous wife, the eagles and the vine, and the fathers and their sons (Ezek. 15–18). His last spoken word was the lament for Israel's princes. So, on at least seven different occasions, Ezekiel has spoken to his fellow exiles within the last several months. Here they stand before Ezekiel again, continuing to seek information, but presumably lacking a change of heart.

READ EZEKIEL 20:1–26.

What did God say He would not allow the elders to do?

To not Inquire

What did God command Ezekiel to do?

Judge the elders

What did God tell the nation of Israel to rid themselves of, and how did they respond?

Detestable things / rebellion

For whose sake did God spare them?

His name

Why does God want us to obey His decrees?

To live

What is God's purpose in giving us a Sabbath?

(Rest) connection between the 2 parties

How does God describe Israel's approach to the Sabbath?

Greatly profaned

What had God commanded the subsequent generation?

To obey

Do not follow forfathers examples

How did they respond, and why did God spare them?

Rebellion / for the sake of his name

After several generations of their refusing to believe God and obey His laws, what did God eventually decide to do?

lead into wilderness

What would the people of Israel know as a result of God's punishment?

That he is God

The nation of Israel had many laws when it came to their worship of God. Some came from God Himself passed down through Moses, and many became added along the way throughout Israel's history. God seems to focus on one law in particular in this rebuke toward the exiles: *they profaned His Sabbath.*

The command of the Sabbath was to take a day of rest. To acknowledge our trust in God to complete His work in our lives, to fulfill His purposes for us, and to provide for us what we need. A Sabbath rest was unique to the God of Israel. The Egyptians, Canaanites, and Persians had gods who commanded to be cared for by their worshipers. Only Yahweh alone was the God who cared for His people. The Sabbath was meant to be a signpost as to the uniqueness of Israel's God—both the greatness of His capabilities as the self-existent, all-sufficient One in need of nothing, but also the kindness of His character, that He cared for the needs of His people. The false gods of the surrounding nations insisted their worshipers strive to attain the gods' favor in hopes they would provide what the people needed. The God of Israel invited His children to rest in His presence and trust His provision in full assurance of both His intent and ability to provide for them.

The Sabbath allows us to reflect and recognize that all we have comes from God. All of our hopes and dreams rest on Him. We remain completely and totally dependent on Him for our existence. We cease striving, trying to figure things out independent of Him, and attempting to accomplish the myriads of tasks set before us through our own effort and strength, and instead be still and know that He is God.

How easy is it for you to rest? Draw an X where you would place yourself on the continuum.

It is easy to let go and trust	*Sometimes I give things over, and other things I try to work out on my own*	*If I'm not actively working, I fret*

I found it so interesting that God said it is through the Sabbath that He sanctifies us, or makes us holy. How might intentionally resting and ceasing all labor provide an opportunity for God to revive our hearts and become more intimate with Him?

[handwritten: physical rest = mental rest]

[handwritten: Time for prayer]

Ezekiel 20:25–26 is a bit confusing. What could God mean when He says, "I gave them statutes that were not good and rules by which they could not have life"? God informs us in this statement that He allowed Israel to chase after her own sinfulness. The people chose to alter God's Laws to suit their preferences, adding in idol worship into the midst of God's prescribed way to worship Him. God had decreed to His people that each firstborn son belonged to Him. He meant it to be a remembrance of how He had spared all of the firstborn sons during the plague on the Egyptians (see Ex. 12:29–30) and also an acknowledgment that it was God who gave life. But the Canaanite god Molech demanded every firstborn son ought to be sacrificed as a burnt offering upon the altar, so the Israelites changed God's Law to emulate their pagan neighbors.

God's desire in allowing the nation of Israel to fall into such depravity was so that they might literally become "sin-sick"; so disgusted by their sinfulness that they would turn to the Lord for cleansing. Clearly, we humans can become horrifically sinful and still lack desire to return to God for restoration.

Paul echoes this tactic of God to hand us over to our depravity. (See Romans 1:1–25.) What hope are we given in Romans 8:10–11?

[handwritten: Christ]

How about your own life? Have you ever experienced a time in your life when a certain sin grew quite comfortable? How did God start to make it distasteful to you?

I'm not sure yet

Has God ever brought you to a moment where you were sickened by your own sin? What did you learn about grace through this experience?

God's desire is to bring us life. The purpose of the Law is to demonstrate how desperate we are without Him. We are utterly dependent on God's grace for life. The purpose of the Sabbath is to reflect on His goodness, provision, and care for us. Let's spend some time thanking Him today. Close your eyes, open your hands, and acknowledge those areas of your life in which you are tightly clinging, trying to secure the outcome you think best. Ask for faith to trust in God's perfect plan and provision for that person or situation.

The exiles wanted Ezekiel to promise them a swift return back home, not the destruction of their homeland and more years in captivity. God's ways are not our own. Revival requires making peace that God's best does not always seem good in our limited human view. But the One who knows the end from the beginning has a plan and a purpose in mind that we cannot see. God's end game was revival—to return His people to their unique purpose: a relationship with Himself through which the world would see the greatness and goodness of Israel's God. The same purpose He has for you and me. Trust Him.

THE SWORD OF THE SILVERSMITH

EZEKIEL 21–22

The time of testing is over. God offers no more opportunities for His people to repent. Nebuchadnezzar's sword will come against Jerusalem, destroying her completely. God's Name would not be profaned. If He was not exalted through His relationship with His people, then His sovereignty and authority would be displayed through the punishment of His people. God specifically makes known His sovereignty in four ways:

1. Through testing. He brings discipline with the rod to bring us to repentance in hopes of not having to bring punishment (21:13).

2. Through a pagan king. Although Nebuchadnezzar sought the direction of his false gods by divination, it was ultimately God who directed his path (21:18–24).

3. Through pagan nations. Nebuchadnezzar would not be allowed to begin his assault upon God's people until He allowed it (21:27).

4. Through the punishment of God's enemies. While the Ammonites may be smug when Nebuchadnezzar pursues the destruction of Jerusalem leaving their city of Rabbah alone, God informs them that their own destruction awaits as well (21:28–32).

Compare God's Ten Commandments with the sins of the people of Jerusalem. Draw a line between God's commands and how they have broken them in Ezekiel 21:6–12:

TEN COMMANDMENTS: EXODUS 20:1–17:	EZEKIEL 22:6–12:
You shall have no other gods before me	Father and mother are treated with contempt
You shall not make for yourself a carved image	The sojourner suffers extortion
You shall not take the Name of the LORD in vain	The fatherless and the widow are wronged
Remember the Sabbath and keep it holy	You have profaned My Sabbaths
Honor your father and mother	Men slander to shed blood
You shall not murder	Eat with idols on the mountains
You shall not commit adultery	Commit lewdness with neighbor's wife, with daughter-in-law, his sister
You shall not steal	Take interest and profit, and make gains from your neighbor by extortion
You shall not covet your neighbor's house or wife	Take bribes and shed blood
You shall not bear false witness	You have forgotten Me

Clearly God had much to be angry over concerning the conduct of His people. What's interesting is that God does not call them evil, wicked, or terrible. He refers to them as dross (see Ezek. 22:17–22). By definition, dross is: "the refuse in impure materials that is generally separated by melting where the dross rises to the top and may then be skimmed off. It is used figuratively of what is worthless."[18] Their purpose was to demonstrate the sovereignty, power, and goodness of God to the world but, in their sin, they had become just like every other nation. There was nothing different about them, nothing to set them apart, meaning they no longer represented God adequately or set Him apart from all other gods.

When we as Christians look and live like everybody else, we profane the cross of Christ. We become useless in pointing others to Him. People don't come to Jesus because He successfully looks and acts like the world, they come to Him because He is not of this world. People need to know there is a better option. Herein lies the problem: from our perspective, our outward behavior appears righteous in comparison to the choices of the world. But God implores us to look within and see the hidden sins of the heart that render us as dross in our efforts to point the world to Jesus: pride, self-righteousness, selfishness, laziness toward our purpose. None of these attitudes represent the gospel or the sacrifice of Christ. The people of the world are not looking for someone to help them clean up their act, they are looking for someone who can make sense of their desperate and chaotic circumstances. They need to see humility, dependence, fervency in purpose, and surrendered lives. God longed to purify Israel just as He longs to do with His church today.

In order for silver to be made into a useful object, the silversmith must melt it down to remove impurities; then it can be cast into the image the silversmith wants to make. When God placed the nation of Israel into the fire, there was nothing useful left in her. She had become so impure, she was worthless dross.

A precious metal like silver doesn't become contaminated and rendered useless overnight. It takes the consistent infiltration of outside minerals, certain natural circumstances, and a long period of time, emphasizing that Israel's dissolution had occurred over consistent exposure to damaging influences.

READ EZEKIEL 22:23–31.

How had each of the groups below contributed to Israel's impurity?

PROPHETS:

PRIESTS:

PRINCES:

PEOPLE:

What is the common thread among all of these groups? They had been chosen by God: set apart from the world and entrusted with the truth of Who God Is to share with the world. *Just like us.*

We have been commanded to share the gospel of truth to a world walking in darkness. As believers in Jesus we are called a "royal priesthood" (see 1 Peter 2:9).

For whom was God searching yet unable to find?

What did God therefore decide to do?

The "breach" in verse 30 refers to a break in a defensive wall usually made by an army attacking. The New International Version of Ezekiel 22:30 uses the word "gap" and renders this verse: "I looked for someone among them who would build up the wall and stand before me in the gap on behalf of the land." The definition of a "gap" is: "an empty space, a lag, a disparity, a separation by breaking."[19] In Christian parlance we often hear the phrase "stand in the gap," used figuratively. What does it mean?

God was looking for someone who would boldly proclaim the disparity between the holiness of God and the current lifestyle choices of the people. God was looking for someone who would emphatically announce the need to break away from the world and be reunited to God. God was looking for someone who was willing to do the hard work of building up the wall, exposing its weakness and strengthening its gaping holes to keep out the enemy. *And He found no one.*

What about today? Sadly, we don't find many pastors calling out our sinfulness contrasting God's perfection and holiness. We see a lot of gospel celebrities who look like an upgraded version of the world, but not a whole lot of self-denying servants. Building a wall is hard work. It takes heavy lifting, constant shaping of rough, hard stones, and the willingness to work with others. I remember walking in the tunnels underground, where the temple had stood in Jerusalem and seeing the stones dating all the way back to Herod's temple. Each one weighed thousands of pounds. No one individual would be able to navigate the repair of a stone that size. It would take many workers collectively to make a difference.

If we are going to be people of whom God says, "There's my girl, standing in the gap," it's going to take commitment. We are going to have to fervently study the Word of God. It will take courage to speak that Word in its fullness. Not just the fuzzy, feel-good promises, but also the hard truths. We will have to commit to fellowship and service with other believers, which gets messy and sometimes painful. When someone else doesn't carry their weight and drops a two–ton rock on your toe, it's going to do some damage. But God searches. Will He find you?

The silversmith knew he was ready to fashion his metal when he looked into the melted pool of silver and saw his own reflection. When after slow and steady fire, all the dross had been surfaced and consistently skimmed away. Only the pure silver remained, reflecting the image of the silversmith who stood examining it. What does God see when He looks at you? Let's pray and ask Him to do as He promised and conform us into the image of His Son.

A TALE OF TWO SISTERS

EZEKIEL 23

Do you remember that old adage "Be careful what you wish for"? It conveys the idea that from the outside it seems that obtaining what we so deeply desire would ensure our happily ever after, but maybe we don't know all that getting it might entail. It goes hand in hand with another adage: "There's always more to the story." The nation of Israel looked at their neighboring nations and wanted what they had. The Assyrian warriors strode handsomely on their horses full of power and allure. The Babylonian merchants flaunted their wealth and array of pleasing goods, and Israel insatiably craved their wares. Instead of remaining set apart from the pagan nations, Israel began to pursue them, wishing to be like them. And it led to their downfall. Israel failed to listen to the rest of the story God kept faithfully reading to them through His prophets.

READ EZEKIEL 23:1–27.

Who do the two sisters represent?

Oholah:

Oholibah:

("Samaria" is the northern kingdom, Israel; and "Jerusalem" is Judah, the southern kingdom.)

What happened to Oholah?

After witnessing the choices of her sister Oholah, what did Oholibah decide to do?

What would happen to Oholibah as a result?

Well, this is a rather explicit tale. *Read Jeremiah 3:8–18. Despite all of this, what did God ultimately long for from His "daughters"?*

Let's make this national history lesson a bit more personal. How does the story of these two sisters relate to you and me? For starters, there is a progression of sin here we cannot miss. First, they were enticed by the power of the Assyrians, then afterward the wealth of the Babylonians. In the end, neither satisfied the desire of their hearts.

Herein lies a documentary of our enemy and the nature of sin. He entices us with something we long to have, in this case power and wealth. It could be the same for us, or it could be pleasure, significance, someone to "love" us, any number of things that he will make us believe we cannot be happy without obtaining them. Once we are enticed, then we will begin to pull our hearts away from God and toward that thing we desire in an effort to gain it.

Satan will try to entice us with anything other than God's best for us. It isn't always a bad thing; it just isn't God's best. Then because God doesn't go along with the program, we begin to pull even further away from Him and exalt our enticements above His desires for us. We begin to listen to and chase after the things of this world to try and get what we want. If we aren't sure God is going to give us that which we so ardently desire, we will listen to other voices to help us figure out a way to gain it.

I've seen it countless times.

- I know I'm not supposed to date a non-Christian but I'm just so lonely.

- I know reading endless romance novels in the midst of my struggling marriage makes me more frustrated with my spouse's emotional distance, but I enjoy the escape.

- I know eating lunch alone in the breakroom with my coworker isn't wise, but he just gets me and he's easy to talk to compared to my husband.

- I know working late and not spending time with my kids isn't good, but I'm just so close to that next promotion or raise.

- I know I shouldn't keep charging items on my credit card in my current financial situation but having something new to wear makes me feel better.

- I know I shouldn't need to have a drink every night before I go to bed but it just helps me sleep better. And I'm so tired.

- I know scrolling through social media or binge-watching TV shows draws me into my own world and away from being fully present with my family, but my mind just needs a rest.

Sometimes God will allow us to get what we were chasing after, and once we get it, guess what happens? We turn away from it in disgust, just like the nation of Judah did. Why? Because it did not deliver the satisfaction we thought it would.

Once we see the enticement as it really is, we are severely disappointed by it, we are angry that it did not give us the thrill that it promised, and we are angry that we were duped by it! Satan deals in illusions and lies. That which he dangles before us never delivers. And the results of obtaining the dangling carrot are never what we anticipate them to be. Once we finally come to this realization, though, God will also allow something else to happen: the consequences that come along with obtaining it.

For the nation of Israel, that included captivity and their widespread destruction. And here's the thing: that enticement the enemy has convinced you that you need? It includes captivity and widespread destruction as well. To your own heart and life as well as all those around you.

READ EZEKIEL 23:28–35.

List every consequence Oholibah would face as a result of her prostitution.

Have you ever longed for something intensely and tried to gain it for yourself without seeking God's direction?

If you did obtain it, what happened?

READ JAMES 1:17.

If something is perfect for us, from whom does it come?

Do you believe that God wants to give you what is perfect for you?

If so, how have you come to that belief, and if not, what keeps you from fully believing Him?

No matter how long we walk with the Lord, we will continue to battle desires that well up within us enticing us to pursue pleasures apart from the Lord. We must constantly be before the Lord in humility, asking Him to give us discernment regarding our desires and to seek Him for direction in them. He desires for us to be His faithful bride who longs to please Him alone!

What does James 4:1–3 warn us about desiring less than God's best for us?

Who or what is your heart chasing after today?

DON'T SHED A TEAR

EZEKIEL 24

Is there anything quite like a promise kept? For twenty-three chapters, and a span of nearly five years, Ezekiel prophesied the destruction of Jerusalem. But only when God loosened his tongue allowing him to speak. The exiles to which he prophesied doubted and questioned him all along. Despite all of God's dramatic word pictures presented to them regarding God's heart for His people, His desire to draw them near to Himself, and His warning of dire consequences, the exiles still did not want to repent. Back in Ezekiel 12:28, God began to inform the exiles that these prophecies given would be imminently fulfilled. And today is the day when God says, "See, I told you so!" In fact, God even commands Ezekiel to write this day down.

READ EZEKIEL 24:1–8.

Record the date that Nebuchadnezzar laid siege to the city of Jerusalem.

Now, please don't forget, the exiles are miles and miles away from the walls of Jerusalem. But another prophet remains inside the city. *What dates does he record for the beginning of the siege in Jeremiah 39:1 and 52:4?*

What phrase does God use to let the exiles know God means right now (Ezek. 24:2)?

What type of story is Ezekiel to tell the exiles?

Who or what do you think the pot and the meat/bones represent? (Look back at Ezekiel 11:3 if you are unsure.)

How does God describe the deposit in the pot?

Listen to this explanation: "In the fire of God's judgment, Jerusalem's 'impurities' floated to the surface. The corruption could not be hidden. She was as unappealing as rusty scum floating on the surface of a meal being cooked. The meal was ruined by the rusty scum, so the contents of the pot were dumped."[20] Since the deposit was permanently part of the pot, it could never be useful for cooking, as it would ruin anything ever placed within it. Everything cooked in it becomes waste. None of the meal is edible, symbolizing that none of the inhabitants of Jerusalem are notable in fulfilling their purpose of being a light to the nations.

In Leviticus 17:13, God commanded the blood of animals to be covered after being poured out. Blood symbolized life, so the murder of the animal needed to be covered. God's commands in this parable emphasize that the death and injustice caused by the inhabitants of Jerusalem would not be hidden. Revenge is on its way.

READ EZEKIEL 24:9–12.

What would happen to the bones and the pot?

God is turning up the heat. Consider this explanation:

> The judgment was to be unusually thorough. The caldron itself was to remain on the fire until it also melted, thus doing away with the rust. That it had been emptied, signified that a full captivity would depopulate the land. Moreover, it was not sufficient that the people only be destroyed; the city itself had to be demolished. There was no mistaking the intention of God; in order to purge the city, He would have to destroy it completely.[21]

We would be wise to ask ourselves, when trials or discipline come into our lives, do we surrender and allow God's cleansing process, or do we frustrate His efforts by continued rebellion allowing the scum of our sin to remain? God had attempted over and over to purify His people and restore them to fulfilling their true calling of bringing Him glory and thus others to Him, but God's people would not listen.

Note this further explanation:

> The nation had proved incorrigible and all pleas had been unavailing, with even preliminary and token punishments having failed to achieve anything of lasting value in the people's spiritual life. The Lord had sought to purge them through the ministry of the prophets, providential dealings and calamities, but nothing procured the desired result. They were now left to the consequences of their evil deeds.[22]

Think through events during your own lifetime. What types of natural calamities or circumstances has the world experienced leaving us feeling a loss of control that could wake people up to their need for God?

How does Paul describe someone who could be comparable to a modern-day prophet in Acts 20:18–21, 27?

READ EZEKIEL 24:15–27.

What does God say is going to happen to Ezekiel's wife?

How is Ezekiel supposed to respond?

What did the people ask Ezekiel regarding this response?

Does anybody else find this to be an extremely difficult passage of Scripture? God has asked some very difficult things of Ezekiel thus far. He has given up his lifelong preparations to serve as a priest in the temple of Jerusalem and has been taken captive as a political prisoner to Babylon, a foreign nation with foreign gods and sinful practices. God took away his ability to speak and only loosens his tongue in order to allow him to utter specific prophetic words from God. He has lain on his side for 430 days, barely eating and drinking. He shaved his head and beard. And for the most part, all of this sacrifice has been rendered ineffective in being used by God to turn the hearts of those to whom God had called him to minister! Wow! How many of us would faithfully endure so much self-sacrifice with such minimal results?

I can remember one cold, wintry morning. I was standing in a still half-asleep state in front of my coffee pot waiting for it to brew when my phone rang. It was still dark and quiet outside, and the jolting ring in my silent house startled me. On the other end of the phone was my dear friend who had called to beg for prayer because she had awoken that morning only to discover she was most likely going to face her fourth miscarriage. Her husband was taking her to the hospital and she desperately needed the peace of God to reign over her heart during this difficult moment, a repeat of a heartbreak she had already experienced three previous times in less than a year. I can remember getting down on my knees in front of my coffee pot pleading with the Lord to let this baby live. I couldn't understand why He would take another child from them. My friend and her husband were strong prayer warriors, faithful servants, and loving, selfless people. Who better to raise a child in this world?

I can remember God speaking to me, not out loud, but in my heart, asking, "Would you be willing to give up your own ability to bear a child in order that your friend might bear many children?" I remember being shocked by the question and asking, "God, why would You ask me that? I don't understand." At which point God gently answered, "You see, that is what I did for you. I gave up My one and only Son in order that I might bear many children for My glory." I understood a bit more deeply what the heart of our Father sacrificed by giving up His Son for me. I also understood that all the emotions and heartache that my friend and her husband were experiencing at that moment had also been experienced by God Himself. God is asking Ezekiel to give up his wife for the sake of His glory. And He is asking Ezekiel not to mourn for her.

But this next part of the narrative pummels my heart the fiercest. Rather than try to mourn for Ezekiel or attend to him in any way, they want to know what this has to do with them. I just want to shout, "*Are you kidding me?*" Ezekiel's wife has just died, he isn't mourning at all, and all the people want to know is, "*What does this have to do with me?*" We always want to make it all about us, don't we? Me, me, me. Our favorite person. Maybe, just maybe, in the wake of Ezekiel's tragedy, the people might finally be ready to listen.

READ EZEKIEL 24:20–27.

What beloved thing of the exiles was about to die?

How were the people commanded to respond?

What would the people know as a result?

The exiles were to stand in agreement with God's holiness and His need to punish Israel. They needed to acknowledge that God's ways, although not what they wanted, were what they needed. We need to ask ourselves how we respond when God turns up the heat in a loved one's life or even our own. Do we frantically smack at the flames, telling God that the fire is just too hot? Or do we step back, trust in His ways, and pray for the Refiner's fire to do its work?

Have you ever had to watch a loved one experience the discipline of the Lord? Or have you experienced the discipline of the Lord yourself? If so, without telling any details that could harm your loved one, how did you feel and what did God teach you through it?

What would Ezekiel be able to do once the city of Jerusalem finally fell?

This marks the end of God speaking judgment over His people. Beginning in chapter 25, God will begin pronouncing judgment on the surrounding nations. What is important to note is that, when it comes to revival, God always deals with His own people first. Healing begins with the prayers of God's people. Revival begins with the repentance of God's people. The spark of the revelation of God's glory begins among us. We must first turn to the Lord inviting Him to ignite His fire of cleansing, purification, and power.

Can you think of a relationship in your life in which you are pleading with God to stop His work because watching it is so painful? How does stepping back and remembering that God holds a different perspective in the situation bring you comfort?

If my people who are called by my name humble themselves,
and pray and seek my face and turn from their wicked ways, then I will
hear from heaven and will forgive their sin and heal their land.

2 CHRONICLES 7:14

REACHING THE WORLD THROUGH REVIVAL

God's Heart for the Nations

LOVE THY NEIGHBOR

EZEKIEL 25–26

Today God will introduce us to five of Israel's neighbors. What we will notice is how God judges each of them for different sins. Not so surprisingly, we will find each of these nations' sins quite relatable to our times today.

READ EZEKIEL 25:1–7.

How did the Ammonites respond to the news of Jerusalem's destruction?

They said, _____ (v. 3). They clapped their ___hands___, stamped their ___feet___ and ___rejoiced___ with all the malice in their soul (v. 6).

What would the Ammonites know once the judgment of God fell upon them through the hands of the Babylonians?

He is God

There is a pattern of God here we cannot miss. God does not simply punish for punishment's sake. No matter how deserving the punishment might be. God punishes for redemption's sake, so that both those who witness and experience the punishment might turn in repentance and return to God. Instead, the Ammonites relished Israel's punishment. When we see God's justice meted out on even those most deserving, do we rejoice, or do we fall on our faces in awe that because of God's great sacrifice on the cross, we will miraculously be spared of such justice ourselves?

READ EZEKIEL 25:8–11.

What did the people of Moab say about Judah?

> Judah became like the other nations

What did God desire the people of Moab to know?

> He is God

God will repeat this desire in speaking of all of Israel's neighbors. Do you think maybe God had in mind to remind His people of their purpose? To show their neighboring nations the uniqueness of Yahweh in comparison to all the other false gods the people futilely worshiped?

The Moabites seethed with jealousy over Israel and her special status as God's chosen people. They, too, were descendants of Abraham, through his nephew Lot, but Israel did not consider them to be heirs of the same promises as the people of Israel. When something bad happens to someone who seems to have special favor or status, do we inwardly smirk due to our jealousy? Or when they mess up do we feel so much better about our own fallibilities? When someone who seemed to be growing like gangbusters starts to spiritually wither do we feel better about our own lack of growth? We don't want anyone else to seemingly have a more intimate, successful, or meaningful relationship with God than we do. This is the sin of Moab.

READ EZEKIEL 25:12–14.

How did God describe Edom's actions toward the house of Judah?

Edom became guilty

What would the people of Edom know about God, and how is that different from the rest of the nations?

Know His Vengeance

The Edomites are also referred to as the nation of Seir, because that is the mountain on which they lived. The Edomites were descendants of Esau, Jacob's older brother. So essentially the Israelites and the Edomites are cousins. Rather than Nebuchadnezzar enacting the Lord's vengeance on Edom, God says the nation of Israel will do it. This breaks the pattern from the previous two being punished via Babylon so we must ask ourselves the reason why.

The only time Israel ever defeated Edom was under King David. When God spoke of Edom being conquered by Israel, the people's ears would have perked up. They would have understood this to be referencing the arrival of the Son of David, that is, the Messiah who was to come. References to Edom in prophetic Scripture seem to refer to the opponents of Israel's Messiah and encompass a spiritual allegiance rather than simply a race or a nationality. Within these three simple verses God reminds the nation of Israel that the promise of the Son of David, the Messiah, has not been forgotten by God.

READ EZEKIEL 25:15–17.

How did the Philistines act toward Israel?

Vengeance   Malice
hostility

What would the Philistines know when God exacted His vengeance on them?

He is God

This people group held no ancestral relation to Israel and were located roughly where Palestine is today. Unlike all the previous people groups mentioned, the Philistines were not descendants of Abraham. In the event that the people of Israel thought they only needed to reveal God's glory to distant relatives, God makes it clear that He desired all people to know Him as Lord.

The sin of the Philistines is that they rejoiced over the punishment of the wicked. What would we rather witness? The punishment of the wicked or to witness them repent and receive mercy? If it is the former and not the latter we have "malice of soul" like the Philistines. This response indicates the pride of Israel. Do we view ourselves as morally or spiritually superior in comparison to those who outwardly appear more wicked than ourselves?

The fifth nation God rebukes includes Tyre. An independent city-state, Tyre consisted of two geographical components, a mainland portion and an island about a half mile off the coast. The two were connected by a bridge. Her sister city was Sidon and the two cities together made up the nation of Phoenicia. This was a nation of mariners. Because Tyre sailed all over the ancient world, they could obtain wares sold solely by them and they therefore became very wealthy. The ships of Tyre could be equated to the world's first floating SuperTarget where you could get anything in the ancient Middle East your heart desired.

READ EZEKIEL 26:1–7.

What did Tyre say regarding Jerusalem?

Jerusalem = Ruins

Tyre = Prosper

How did God respond?

Not happy

Tyre plundered

The nation of Israel held a long history with Tyre and Sidon. When David established himself as king over the nation of Israel, Hiram, king of Tyre, sent supplies and laborers for David to build a palace for himself as the newly established king (see 2 Sam. 5:11). Tyre was able to sail all around to the many continents to achieve wares, but once they returned to their port on the Mediterranean, the Tyrians needed to travel inland to trade them. David, being the king of Israel, controlled the inland trade routes, so it was a win-win for these two kings to form an alliance. Because Tyre was geographically small, she also depended on the agrarian Israelites for food supplies.

David's son Solomon continued to be on friendly terms with Hiram, and during Solomon's reign, the king of Tyre provided laborers and supplies for the construction of God's temple in Jerusalem (1 Kings 5). When the nation of Israel split into northern Israel and southern Judah, Tyre and Sidon partnered with the northern Israel. In order to secure this continued alliance, Ahab, king of Israel, married Jezebel, daughter of Ethbaal, king of the Sidonians (1 Kings 16:31). So, for a long time, Tyre had depended on the nation of Israel to be able to travel through her inland trade routes in order to sell their imports and obtain their wealth. The Israelites would have levied taxes on Tyre and Sidon in order for them to do so. Now that Jerusalem had fallen, they no longer depended on her, and in their greed thought they would now become even wealthier.

The prophet Ezekiel signals God's desire for global evangelism most brightly. Over and over God explains His desire for these surrounding nations to know that He is the One True God—high above all other false gods of wood and stone. He is the covenant-keeping, relational God who will woo His people with provision and punish for apostasy.

The people of Jerusalem never expected their city to be destroyed, because they relied on God's protection of it. The people of the world thought that Tyre could never be destroyed because of its immense wealth and geographical location. It was protected on one side by mountains and, though the other portion was an island, it was heavily guarded by its vast merchant fleet. They thought they were invincible, and the rest of the ancient world thought so too. The surrounding nations would think: "If Tyre can fall, then who can possibly stand?" The destruction of Tyre offers a stark image of the frailty and futility of man against the power and purposes of God.

We will examine this ancient city even further tomorrow, but the question that remains for us today is this: Are we showing our neighbors Who God Is and what He is like? Or are we pridefully hoarding our special status as His chosen people?

THERE IS NO GOD LIKE JEHOVAH

EZEKIEL 27

The city of Tyre smugly relished the destruction of Jerusalem. God essentially tells them, "The same fate is coming to you, Tyre, so get ready!" God will not be mocked. It actually took Nebuchadnezzar thirteen years to defeat Tyre, because even though he laid siege to the mainland portion of the city, the island portion remained able to ferry in fresh food supplies. God had a purpose behind this lengthy siege, which we will cover next week in the study. As I read Scripture alongside historical accounts of other writers, I am continually amazed at the purpose and precision of God and His Word!

Nebuchadnezzar did defeat the mainland portion of the city but never captured the island. History further tells us that under the Tyrian conquest by Alexander the Great in 332 BC, he built a causeway between the mainland and the island by throwing rocks into the sea, leaving the city bare. Once the causeway was constructed, he then rode across it with his army and invaded and destroyed the island portion of Tyre.[23] A half-mile-long causeway across the sea sounds like a good place for fishermen to labor and then dry out their nets, doesn't it?

It is important to note these prophecies for two purposes. One, because when we can historically see the fulfillment of God's Word in such detailed precision, it bolsters our faith. When we know God's promises are rock solid throughout the millennia, we become emboldened to trust the character of God today. The Bible is a book about God: His capabilities and His character. Knowing His power, purposes, and faithfulness help us trust Him in our quaking circumstances and critical decisions. We have a faithful Father holding us tightly as He unfolds our future.

Second, we note these prophecies, because it appears they represent two different time periods in history. Historically we see these prophecies did not become entirely fulfilled through Nebuchadnezzar, but this should not entirely surprise us, because there is also a shift in Ezekiel's linguistic structure that further clarifies that the entirety of this prophecy will be fulfilled at two different times. Look carefully at Ezekiel 26:8, 9, 10, 11 and notice the pronoun he uses at the beginning of each of these verses. Now look at verse 12. Do you see the shift from "he" to "they"? Ezekiel clues us in that he is talking about two different invaders.

What additional prophecy did Ezekiel make about Tyre in Ezekiel 26:14?

Never Rebuilt

The Romans actually rebuilt the city of Tyre, and there are New Testament references to its existence (Matt. 15:21; Luke 6:17; Acts 12:20). I do not want you to miss what Ezekiel does here, because he will do the same thing again in his prophecies regarding the king of Tyre. There will be a right now, a sometime later, and a much, much later prophecy all given within the same oracle.
This circles back to the first point: the Bible is a book about God. Prophecy revolves around Christ. In similar structure to Daniel's prophecies, we often see prophets speak of something that will occur within the prophet's own lifetime, authenticating themselves as a true prophet of God; something that will occur when the Messiah arrives; and something that will be fulfilled in the last days or

upon Jesus' return to earth. Three separate time periods of prophecy all predicted within the same oracle.

As far as the permanent destruction of Tyre in verse 14, scholars have suggested different interpretations as to what God meant. Some suggest it to be prophetic hyperbole and not to be taken literally. This interpretation does not fit with the exactness of detail God offers in the rest of this passage, such as the city becoming a place for fishermen to spread or dry their nets (v. 14). Others claim that while the surrounding areas of Tyre were rebuilt, the city itself on its exact location never was.[24] In the thirteenth century, Tyre was held under Muslim rule and was attacked by the Crusaders. The city was completely destroyed into a pile of rubble. Today it is a rather small fishing village in Lebanon, and the exact location of the ancient city remains unknown.

When reading prophetic writing, we need to examine the text carefully for linguistic clues from the prophet as to a break in events even within the same word. In verse 21, when God speaks of the utter end of Tyre, that does not become fulfilled under Nebuchadnezzar's rule. History tells us that after Tyre was defeated by the Babylonians, it was then given over to the Persians and the Syrians. There was a great amount of racial intermarriage among the people of Tyre with all of these subsequent ruling cultures, which led to the virtual nonexistence of a unique Tyrian people.[25] This may be what Ezekiel references here.

The linguistic structure changes again in Ezekiel 26:17–18 and constitutes a funeral dirge.[26] God emphasizes the permanency of the destruction of the city. Just as death is irreversible, so is God's judgment on Tyre. Consider this explanation:

> Just as the Lord God had expressed sorrow of heart over the sin and defection of Israel, He now through Ezekiel set forth a lamentation over the illustrious city of Tyre. God's heart is always moved for the destruction of the ungodly. The doom and sentence of Tyre were viewed as already executed.[27]

Read Ezekiel 27:10–25 and list a few of the items Tyre bartered and sold across the world on their sailing vessels:

> Silver Iron lead tin
> slaves bronze horses and mules

According to Ezekiel 27:33–36, how do the kings of the earth respond to Tyre's demise?

> Shudder with horror
> Distorted with fear

The record of the nation of Tyre holds particular relevance for us today. Tyre represented the wealthiest nation in the ancient world and excelled in the same areas every modern nation seeks to obtain superiority today: in trade, dominance, and wealth. But Tyre's message is the same for us today: all the wealth of the world cannot satisfy. While the mightiest of nations are no match against the power of the Almighty, worldly wealth and dominance drag us away from dependence on God. Has not this same spirit invaded our own nation as well as the lives of too many believers today?

Why do you think the riches and pleasures of the world hold so much temptation for us?

> Provides comfort and power

How do you think an abundance of riches thwarts our view of deep dependence on God?

> Can start to depend on wealth instead

Have you ever gone through a season of life when you had to more deeply depend on God to supply your daily needs? If yes, describe the scenario, and share what you learned.

Nah don't feel like it

Look at Jesus' words in Matthew 6:25–33. Why do you think worries over food, clothing, and daily provisions consume our thoughts?

They are necessities to live
if needs aren't meant we'll die

What does Jesus promise will happen if we seek Him first?

Needs will be fulfilled

Do you believe Jesus when He says this? How does our belief/unbelief influence how we handle our resources? ↑ yes

Faith in Christ will satisfy

I want to point out something here in contrast to God's judgment of Israel. God never condemns Tyre for her business practices. Unlike Israel, whom He cites as oppressive and unjust in her dealings, God never criticized Tyre for either her wealth or her business practices with other nations. We are informed that her rise in wealth "enriched the kings of the earth" (Ezek. 27:33). She brought both wealth and ingenuity to the nation of Israel, especially in the construction of the temple. Tyre represented the most prosperous and advanced society of the ancient world.[28]

The sin of Tyre was her pride and her greed. She relished in her status and she flaunted her wealth. She did not give glory to God for the blessings she experienced, but took all the glory for herself or attributed it to her false gods of wood and stone. In the people's minds she was a self-made city. When we begin to view our resources as things that *we* own, have earned by *our* labor, or have acquired through *our* wisdom and ingenuity, then we are committing the sin of Tyre.

According to David in Psalm 24:1, who actually owns all of our stuff?

God

What does Paul admonish the believers in 1 Timothy 6:6–10 regarding our possessions?

Be content

What had happened to some of the early Christians because they had been distracted by the pursuit of riches?

Temptation

fell into harmful desires

The pride and greed of Tyre resulted in her destruction and the world watched in horror over her fall. Will the world watch the church in awe and wonder over her humility and generosity or hiss over her hyprocrisy and self-righteousness?

If we are going to endure to the end, we need revival. If we live in America, we are rich indeed in comparison to the rest of the world.

As for the rich in this present age, charge them not to be haughty, nor to set their hopes on the uncertainty of riches, but on God, who richly provides us with everything to enjoy. They are to do good, to be rich in good works, to be generous and ready to share, thus storing up treasure for themselves as a good foundation for the future, so that they may take hold of that which is truly life.

1 TIMOTHY 6:17–19

BLESSED TO BE A BLESSING

EZEKIEL 28

We need to make the connection once again between God's blessing on Tyre and its resulting blessing on Israel specifically, but also upon the entire ancient world. We are told that when their wares came from the seas, the Tyrians satisfied many peoples, and many nations became enriched through them. We might ask why God would choose to bless a pagan nation rather than Israel herself, but if we understand that this blessing beautifully overflowed to God's chosen people it makes more sense. It also reminded them that Israel's God remained sovereign over all the kings of the earth.

My father was one of the most generous people I have ever met. When he first fell ill, I helped my mom with their finances. My father paid all the bills with a good old-fashioned checkbook, so stacks of mail came into his mailbox each day. I had never realized how many missions organizations, foundations, and causes he supported. Dozens of checks were written monthly to medical research, veterans aid, Christian missionaries, facilities running faith-based programs, so many causes I could not cite them all. When I asked him how many of them he wanted me to continue to support he simply said, "As long as you hold a checkbook with my name on it, write the checks. We are blessed to be a blessing, Erica."

READ EZEKIEL 28:1–10.

Did the king of Tyre view himself as "blessed to be a blessing"?

To what did the king of Tyre attribute his success?

To whom is his wisdom compared (a contemporary of Ezekiel)?

What did God say would happen to the king of Tyre?

Remember those shifts in prophetic structure we talked about yesterday? We are seeing another one here. There are elements of this next portion of prophecy clearly unable to be attributed to a human king.

READ EZEKIEL 28:11–19.

What word here does Ezekiel insert at the beginning to give us a clue that he is expanding his oracle beyond the current king of Tyre?

Look carefully at verse 17. What was this king's overarching sin?

The sin of Satan is pride (1 Tim. 3:6). While the prophecy is directed toward the king of Tyre, there are clearly elements that seem to be attributable to someone beyond this current king. Place a check mark next to some of those attributes below:

You were present in the garden of Eden

You were an anointed guardian cherub

You resided on the holy mountain of God

You walked over stones of fire

Consider this explanation:

> He (Ezekiel) appeared to have the situation of his day in mind with his attention riveted upon the ruler of Tyre, the embodiment of the people's pride and godlessness. But as he viewed the thoughts and ways of that monarch, he clearly discerned behind him the motivating force and personality who was impelling him in his opposition to God. In short, he saw the work and activity of Satan, whom the King of Tyre was emulating in so many ways.[29]

We see a similar thing happen in the teachings of Jesus. *Read Matthew 16:13–23.*
What did Jesus say to Peter?

Looking carefully at the beginning of verse 21, and note the first three words.
What "time" does Matthew refer to? It was the moment after Jesus had just
made something unequivocally clear to His disciples. What was it?

So Peter had just acknowledged that Jesus was the promised Messiah. Barely a
moment later Jesus calls him Satan. Ouch! Jesus does not mean that Peter is Satan
himself. Rather, He implies that Peter's refusals to have Jesus suffer and die are
motivated by Satan. Ezekiel's prophecy against the king of Tyre is similar. Satan is
behind the motivation, thoughts, and desires of the Tyrian king as well. "Ezekiel
is describing Satan who was the true 'king' of Tyre, the one motivating the human
'ruler' of Tyre."[30]

Do you remember what a lament is? A funeral song. When does one sing a funeral
song? When death has come. The destruction of Tyre is certain. The destruction of
Satan and his world order is sure. What God has spoken will come to pass. As we
have studied thus far, many of Ezekiel's prophecies have been fulfilled throughout
history with incredible specificity. We can trust that Satan's ultimate fall and
destruction will come to pass as well.

Blessed to be a blessing. Satan had been created perfect in beauty to be the
guardian cherub of the garden of Eden, but instead of giving God glory and
fulfilling his purpose, he tried to become like God and take the garden for himself.
Who knows? Maybe he had become jealous over Adam and Eve and their special
relationship with God. For a time, he has been given the riches and beauty and

wealth of this world, but that time will come to an end and it will be restored to the One to whom it rightfully belongs.

We, too, are blessed to be a blessing. With what has God blessed you? What are your spiritual gifts? What other talents has He bestowed upon you? Time? Resources? Knowledge and experiences? Are you willing to allow God to bless the world through you or are you continuing to insist you have nothing to offer?

Such a deprecating view of ourselves is nothing more than a twisted form of pride. Your limited, tainted view of yourself attempts to trump the truth of God's view of you and purposes in His creation of you. Blessed to be a blessing. Go out and bless someone today. Taking our eyes off ourselves is the first step toward repentance and revival.

Who is God laying on your heart to bless today?

THE TROUBLE WITH EGYPT

EZEKIEL 29

I remember purchasing my first car right after I graduated from college. Up until that point I never noticed that particular make and model very often, but once I chose a Honda Accord as my vehicle of choice, I suddenly saw them everywhere. In a loose parallel we could suggest God sees His chosen people in a similar manner. Once He chose the nation of Israel, everywhere He looked He noticed His chosen children. Everything and everyone else became filtered through the view of His chosen people. Which is why when it comes to prophecies regarding Israel's neighbors, He does not cite them in order of occurrence, He speaks them in order of impact. Israel's oldest and most influential neighbor had been Egypt. It was also the farthest away geographically. God started His prophecies through Ezekiel to Israel's neighbors in closest proximity and works His way outward. Since Egypt is the farthest away geographically from the apple of His eye, Israel, God saves the land of Pharaoh until last.

READ EZEKIEL 29:1–5.

According to verse 1, at what duration of Ezekiel's captivity was this prophecy uttered?

Go back and reread Ezekiel 26:1 and record at what time the prophecy against Tyre was given.

By grouping the prophecies in the manner that he does, Ezekiel emphasizes that the nation of Israel is the central and most important nation to the Lord and the fate of all other nations revolve around her.

What did Pharaoh claim to have made?

How is making such a claim an indirect way of claiming to be God?

What would God do as a result of Pharaoh making such a claim?

And what would the people know as a result?

God uses quite a bit of imagery here, so let's make sure we understand this. The fish to which Ezekiel refers are the people of Egypt. God indicates that the power of Egypt came from the life-giving Nile River where Pharaoh dwelt. God would hurl him from the Nile along with the Egyptians.

READ EZEKIEL 29:6–16.

What type of plant did God call the nation of Egypt?

For how long would Egypt remain desolate?

How does God describe the nation of Egypt after forty years?

God was going to use the nation of Egypt as a permanent object lesson for the nation of Israel. In what way was the nation of Egypt to serve as a reminder to the people of Israel?

What would the people of Israel know when they looked at the nation of Egypt in her lowly state?

Back in Ezekiel 17, God condemned King Zedekiah of Israel for soliciting the help of Pharaoh in rebelling against Nebuchadnezzar. God told the exiles back then that Egypt would prove to be of no help to them, because God had ordained the city of Jerusalem to fall into Nebuchadnezzar's hands. The prophet Jeremiah, who was residing in Jerusalem at the time, also warned King Zedekiah against breaking his covenant with the Babylonians. Pharaoh and his army set out toward Jerusalem to aid the city currently under siege by Nebuchadnezzar, but they ended up turning around, and while the siege was lifted momentarily, the Babylonians (Chaldeans) would still overtake them (Jer. 37:7–10). The people had leaned on Egypt as their staff, but in the end, she was as weak as the tall reeds that grew along the edge of the Nile, offering no support to Israel in her time of desperate need.

In looking to Egypt for help, the nation of Israel was indeed grasping at straws. A reed was like a tall blade of grass, unable to support any weight, blown to and fro by the wind, and easily snapped in two. Oftentimes in our rebellion we would rather rely on the flimsiest of tangibles rather than wait on our almighty God whose ways can be difficult to decipher and understand. God's desire was that the nation of Israel would turn to Him for their help and support.

Read Jeremiah 17:5–8. Describe the man who trusts in other people for strength.

Now describe the man who trusts in the Lord:

Why do you think it is our natural response to look to the wisdom and the aid of man over the limitless power and wisdom of God?

When we seek the counsel and assistance of others over seeking God Himself first through His Word and prayer, what does that say about our belief in God?

God's desire is that we would understand Him to be sovereign. There is nothing in our realm of circumstances or situations that is beyond His reach or ability. When you are in desperate need of wisdom or help, cry out to Him first. He is your most reliable and trustworthy aid.

Read Psalm 142. In David's deepest moment of desperation, of what was he assured?

In this next prophecy of Ezekiel, we fast-forward about seventeen years. God is giving Ezekiel a follow-up prophecy regarding the one he had just given. In the previous prophecy, the exiles are told that God would punish Egypt for her great pride in believing that she had created the Nile River and for aiding the nation of Israel against the Babylonians. In this prophecy, God gives an additional reason for giving Egypt over to the Babylonians.

READ EZEKIEL 29:17–21.

Why was God going to give Egypt over to Nebuchadnezzar?

We discussed back in Ezekiel 26 how Nebuchadnezzar did not fully defeat the city of Tyre. He laid siege to it for thirteen years, but due to their ability to ferry in food from the island portion of the city, the siege lasted much longer than usual. Once Nebuchadnezzar finally captured the mainland portion of the city after so many years, they found it desolate. The Tyrians had fled over to the island and escaped via their sailing vessels. This left a tired and weary Babylonian army with no plunder. God will send them to Egypt to gain spoils of war.

In 572 BC, the Babylonians attacked Egypt and carried off many exiles and possessions. God says of Nebuchadnezzar in regard to his defeat of the Egyptians and bounty of war spoils: "I have given him the land of Egypt as his payment for which he labored, because they worked for me" (Ezek. 29:20). I bet Neb didn't see it that way. I bet he thought he was a self-made man just like the king of Tyre and the pharaoh of Egypt. Pride is pretty hard to shackle in our moments of great success.

God concludes this prophecy by alluding to the fact that He already has plans for a new ruler to arise. Look carefully at verse 21: What did God say He was making for the house of Israel?

A horn was a symbol of strength. Ezekiel was able to speak freely when this prophecy becomes fulfilled. Jerusalem had already fallen to Babylon nearly fifteen years before. As the years have passed, more and more of Ezekiel's previous prophecies have come into fulfillment. Thus, his prophetic words were authenticated and his subsequent prophecies more greatly heeded. Ezekiel has served as a prophet of God for over seventeen years. It's always great to flip to the end and read the happy ending, but before we stay here too long, we are going to have to back up again tomorrow and read some more imminent prophecies regarding the nation of Egypt first.

Let's think about the prophecies pertaining to us as believers in Jesus. We know the happy ending, don't we? Jesus is going to return. If we die before He arrives, we will be ushered into His presence in heaven. We need not fear death. But in the meantime, we still experience the heartache and horrors of living in this fallen world. And we also know that while we shall rejoice at Jesus' return, those who do not know Him will weep and wail and mourn because their opportunity for repentance will have passed. Will we mourn for the lost world that continues to worship their false gods of power, pleasure, and prosperity? Will we pause and remember God's promises to punish His enemies as readily as His promises to protect us? Will we be agents leading others on the pathway to peace with God through our Lord Jesus Christ?

When our care for eternity exceeds our care for the immediate, the sparks of revival are beginning to flicker.

THE TROUBLE WITH EGYPT, CONTINUED

EZEKIEL 30–31

Back in Ezekiel 29, we had two prophecies against Egypt dated approximately seventeen years apart. We are going to look at the rest of the prophecies against Egypt, which are sandwiched in between these first two. At this point, Ezekiel had prophesied to the exiles that Jerusalem would be laid siege by the Babylonians, that the Egyptians would come to their aid, but their assistance would prove fruitless, and that the city would fall into Nebuchadnezzar's hands. So far, Jerusalem is under siege, the Egyptians have come to help, and while Nebuchadnezzar goes out to fight the Egyptians, the siege is temporarily lifted.

God then moves forward and tells the exiles that He will use the sword of Nebuchadnezzar to bring judgment on all of the surrounding nations as well (Ezek. 25–28). Basically, this tells the exiles that Babylon is on the rise to becoming the next world power and they should not make any plans to return back to their homeland any time soon. Because prophecy is meant to glorify God as we read yesterday, God is going to give specific details in His prophecies against Egypt. It is in the fulfillment of these details throughout history that we come to the realization that God is indeed sovereign in the affairs of humankind.

READ EZEKIEL 30:13–19.

List the cities of Egypt God mentions in these verses:

These cities not only constituted the full range of Egypt geographically, symbolizing the totality of the nation being destroyed, but these particular cities also constituted the primary religious centers of the gods of Egypt. God not only is ruler over Pharaoh, but He is sovereign over all of Pharaoh's gods.

What will the people of Egypt know after Nebuchadnezzar defeats them?

Something interesting about the timing of this prophecy is that it most likely occurred near the time of Passover, April of 587 BC.[31] In the history of Israel, Passover was the holiday that the people celebrated in commemoration of their miraculous delivery from Egypt under Moses' leadership. If the exiles had any notions that God was going to do a miracle of deliverance on this Passover, Ezekiel quickly dispelled any such ideas.

Note to Israel: Pharaoh's not coming back to help you. Two months later, Ezekiel's tongue is loosened yet again, and he utters another prophecy against

Egypt. The city of Jerusalem is still under siege by Babylon. Nebuchadnezzar has not fully defeated Egypt yet. That will not occur for another fourteen years. He has just driven the Egyptians back to their own country. Ezekiel makes it clear, however, that Babylon will eventually attack Egypt as well. Even though Egypt considers themselves to be invincible, God will deliver her into the hands of the Babylonians. To talk Egypt down from her pride, God gives Ezekiel a history lesson to share with them.

READ EZEKIEL 31:1–3.

To which nation does God compare Egypt?

According to Ezekiel 31:9–12, who made Assyria beautiful and bountiful and who would eventually destroy her? For what reason would she be punished?

There's that pattern of pride again. Tyre, Egypt, and Assyria. All brought down by pride. Currently, Nebuchadnezzar is being raised up by the hand of God, but he also will be brought low. God desires to drive home the point that He is the only one who is ultimately in control of this world. He sees the heart of every nation and knows who He will raise up and who He will take down. Nothing lies outside of His sovereignty.

One sure sign of pride is when we begin to devise our own schemes or Plan Bs in response to God's plans. This shouts our distrust of God's wisdom and His capabilities. We question if He can actually make good on His promises and if He will be good on our behalf. We question His power and discount His character. Eventually even Nebuchadnezzar made this mistake.

Read Daniel 4:28–37. What did Nebuchadnezzar say about the Lord after God showed him the futility of his pride?

Read Psalm 25:8–9. What is the promise God gives to the humble?

Those who walk in pride God will humble. I don't know about you, but I'm pretty sure I would rather just bend my knees myself. Why don't we close with that today? Bend your knees, bow your head, and humble your heart before God. Acknowledge your utter desperation for Him to even allow you to take your next breath. Confess any areas of your life where pride may have crept in. Ask Him to search your heart. Then spend some time praising Him for His greatness today.

SCENES OF REVIVAL!

God's Heart for His People

THE
WATCHMAN

EZEKIEL 33

In *My Utmost for His Highest*, Oswald Chambers writes, "Never forget what the Lord was like when you were nearest to Him."[32] God called Ezekiel to become a prophet with two miraculous visions and ushered him into the very throne room of God. At this time God spoke. "I have made you a watchman for the house of Israel" (Ezek. 3:17).

Six years have now passed. Ezekiel's tongue remained stuck to the roof of his mouth except when God loosened it to utter prophecies to the people with him in exile. For six long years Ezekiel faithfully warned his fellow exiles of God's judgment on Jerusalem and the surrounding nations. Through Ezekiel, God offered an invitation to return to Him in repentance, that He might take the exiles and return them to the land. God raised up Nebuchadnezzar to be His instrument of wrath and punishment against the wickedness of the world.

The exiles, however, chose not to believe any of this. They could not fathom God allowing the destruction of His temple and desolation of His land. I cannot imagine how overwhelmed Ezekiel must feel. In my humanness I would want to shout, "If you would just listen to what God is telling all of us and repent, He will bring life and restoration to you, but you refuse to listen!" (Said every mother of a teenager at least once in her life, I'm sure.) How tempting it would be to just give up. It is in these moments when God gently comes in and reminds us Who He Is and what He has called us to do. He gives us a fresh vision and inspiration. As my mentor often reminds me, "When you're in the dark, never forget what God showed you in the light."

We all get discouraged. We all lose our way and wonder what God is doing and how we fit into His mysterious plans. Or we followed Him believing He was taking us in a certain direction only to find an unexpected detour that left us disillusioned. Maybe Ezekiel wrestled with wondering whether all his obedience to God would be for naught. His contemporary Jeremiah certainly must have felt that way with no one heeding his warnings while the city was destroyed before his very eyes. All the difficult things both of these men endured to show their people how greatly God longed for them to be restored. But they would not listen.

God in His great faithfulness never leaves us in our doubt and discouragement. He opens our eyes, giving us renewed vision when we seek His will for our lives. It often comes through a fresh revelation from His Word. It could be something we have read a thousand times, but in this particular moment or circumstance, the Words fall afresh bringing hope to a weary soul.

I pray that as you continue to make your way through Ezekiel's prophecies God renews your vision. That your purpose here is to be a light to a dark world: to extend an invitation to the world to turn and live through the death of Christ. To help people understand God's desire for them to know that He is the Lord.

READ EZEKIEL 33:1–9.

Describe the role of the watchman for a city.

What does God remind Ezekiel of in this passage?

God renews Ezekiel's vision and reminds him of his call: to warn the people of impending judgment and invite them to repent and return to God. We, too, have been called to be watchmen of the great and awesome day of the Lord when Christ will return to judge the earth. Do we take this role seriously, or do we shrug our shoulders and say something like "The people surrounding me do not have any interest in God anyway, so I'll just save my breath"?

Have you ever watched that game show *Family Feud*? I used to love to watch that program. A category comes up, and the contestants have to give their top five answers for that category in order to win the round. Let's play our own Family Feud for a moment. *How would you answer this category? Top Five Reasons Why Christians Don't Share Their Faith:*

1.

2.

3.

4.

5.

I imagine our answers might vary a little from person to person, but the gist of them are probably pretty close: fear of rejection, fear of being asked something we don't know how to answer. We convince ourselves they don't really want to hear about Jesus anyway. Or we tell ourselves we don't have a right to "preach" at them because we are so messed up ourselves. Sometimes as believers we can so effectively insulate ourselves from the world that we don't even have any relationships with unbelievers. But one of the top answers I have heard in just about every church I've ever attended is this one: "That's just not my gift."

Ezekiel certainly could have pulled any of the top five cards above. He experienced rejection. He knew the people did not want to hear his words. I'm sure for every prophecy he uttered he had a hundred questions in his mind about what the warnings all meant. Yet God insisted: Hear the word I speak, and give them warning from Me (Ezek. 33:7).

READ EZEKIEL 33:10–20.

How did the exiles describe their sins?

How did the people respond to God's call to repentance?

Look carefully at verse 13. This gives us insight into the hearts of the people. In whom or what were they choosing to trust?

I can almost guarantee that if we went out to any public place in America and began to share God's plan of salvation with someone who was willing to even acknowledge the existence of God and an afterlife, they would have this mentality. It goes something like this: *I am basically a good person. When I die, God is going to look at all of the good things I did, and if the good things outweigh the bad, then I'm going to get into heaven. Or, He will excuse the bad things I did as long as there are more good things than bad overall.* The problem with this mentality? Verse 13 states it explicitly: they are trusting in their own righteousness.

The root of this mentality goes back to the sin of Israel and her surrounding neighbors: *pride.* They can cover themselves and secure their own ticket to heaven. They do not need to cast themselves on God's mercy alone. They can be good enough on their own. They would rather die in their sin than admit their incapability and need for total dependence on God. To have to rely on God's mercy alone seems unjust to them.

To those of us who know the heart of our Father, we cannot understand this mentality. We think to ourselves, "What a relief! I don't have to worry if I'm good enough!" But to confess our inadequacy requires humility, and some would rather hold on to their pride, even if that means eternal death.

If we have been in church a long time we can begin to develop the attitude that this is all "old news" and we know we are only saved by Christ's death and resurrection. But do we live our daily lives as though we truly believe that? If we believe that apart from Christ there is no hope of salvation, then our hearts ought to break for those who have yet to hear of this hope. Why then are we unwilling to face rejection or humiliation and speak of Jesus out in the world? Would we not live in an attitude of repentance daily if we believe that apart from Christ within us we have no righteousness of our own? Why do we allow sin to creep into our lives and grow comfortable with it rather than confess it? Instead, we become more focused on our current circumstances than the eternal state of the souls surrounding us.

READ EZEKIEL 33:21–29.

Where did the "fugitive" come from, and what news did he deliver?

Who had already told Ezekiel this news and when?

What happened when Ezekiel heard it?

Upon what were the people claiming they relied to regain possession of their land? (Look closely at verse 24.)

What does God accuse them of relying on? (See verse 26.)

What did God say would "come to an end"?

Record the first nine words of verse 29:

The news of Jerusalem's fall reached the exiles almost eighteen months after it had happened. Look back at Ezekiel 24:25–27. What did God promise He would do once the city fell?

The city had fallen almost a year and a half before, yet the Israelites still in the land were plotting to retake it by their own strength. Pride remained. When we come to the point where we know that He is the Lord, we renounce all pride. God informed Ezekiel what the remaining inhabitants of Jerusalem were saying. Now God will inform Ezekiel what his fellow exiles were saying to themselves.

READ EZEKIEL 33:30–33.

What did the exiles do in their hearts and minds with the prophecies Ezekiel spoke to them?

However, once the complete destruction of the city of Jerusalem occurred, what would the exiles finally realize?

Have you ever had a person in your life and you wondered, "How far will they have to fall before they finally get it?" Maybe the person you thought of was you. God informs Ezekiel that it will take the complete and total destruction of Jerusalem and all of the remaining Jews who live there before they get it. But even in spite of reporting to the exiles God's judgment on Israel, the exiles still do not repent. They refuse to believe. They seek the words of Ezekiel out of curiosity and complacency rather than concern over their own sin. We, too, can fall into the habit of going to church week after week to seek words to entertain, or comfort us, but walk out with little to no change in our lives. Do we go to church in hopes of being challenged and changed or solely in hopes of being consoled?

We can take this even a step further. Is our primary purpose only to be changed? Should our own holiness be our primary aim? God does not transform us merely to showcase us. He changes us so we are equipped and empowered to go change the world. To become His witnesses. To erase the top five reasons why Christians do not share their faith, because we become people who cannot keep silent. We become like Peter and John who, when threatened even with punishment of imprisonment for talking about Jesus, emphatically stated, "We cannot but speak of what we have seen and heard" (Acts 4:20).

Our quest for sanctification cannot stop with a focus on ourselves. We seek to be changed that we might speak of Jesus with boldness and confidence no matter who or what comes against us. We become brave watchmen warning the world of the destruction that awaits them and offer them the same invitation God offered through Ezekiel: "Turn to Me and live! Why should you die?" Do not get discouraged, dear one, by those who refuse to listen. God will reveal Himself in due time. The rejection or ridicule we face today may result in an eternity of gratitude from a soul rescued from death.

HEADING OUT TO PASTURE

Growing up in the concrete suburbia of greater Los Angeles, I am as ignorant of farm life as you can get. The only animals I ever saw as a child were the ones in the zoo! I don't know much about sheep. Or shepherding. But the little I do know helps me understand what God is getting at in this passage. One of the most enlightening books I have ever read is *A Shepherd Looks at Psalm 23* by W. Phillip Keller, and it's considered a classic. The author was a shepherd by trade and walks the reader through exactly what David meant when he sang this famous psalm. The things I remember most from reading the book? Sheep are smelly and dumb! Without their shepherd constantly guiding and protecting them, they get lost, they fall off cliffs, and they wander away. They also are extremely auditory. They learn the sound of their shepherd's voice, and then they listen for it.

The shepherd was responsible for the well-being of the sheep entrusted to his care. Most often he was a hired man and the sheep did not in fact belong to him. David was the shepherd of his father Jesse's sheep. He was also the youngest sibling. Guarding the sheep probably was not the most sought-after chore within his household. He slept outside on the ground if he needed to take the flock too far away to return home. He fought against bears and other wild animals who might attack the sheep. Hanging out in the middle of a bunch of smelly sheep is not the job I would volunteer for when the chores were divvied up!

The Israelites were farmers and very familiar with sheep. They owned sheep and animals all the way back to Abraham. Sheep constituted an integral part of their worship of God, because the high priest would sacrifice a lamb each year on the Day of Atonement. And let us not forget the Passover celebrated annually, with the perfect lamb slaughtered for their sins. The "shepherds" of Israel figuratively represented the priests, scribes, elders, and leaders of the people, and ultimately the king. So, when Ezekiel gives the people the sheep and shepherds analogy, he isn't talking to a Los Angeles city slicker like me. He is talking to people who have been around sheep their entire lives. Some of them may even have been shepherds themselves.

READ EZEKIEL 34:1–24.

Why is God angry at the shepherds?

WHAT THE SHEPHERDS DID DO	WHAT THE SHEPHERDS DID NOT DO

What was the result of their poor shepherding?

Who would God send to care for His sheep instead?

Record as many promises as you can find in this passage regarding what God says He will do for His sheep:

Does the Lord let the people off the hook for their foolishness since they had such bad shepherds?

What is God's remedy for the behavior of the sheep?

Who would ultimately rule over them?

God lays the groundwork for the coming of Christ. Jesus, God Himself clothed in human flesh, would gather His sheep as the Good Shepherd. The shepherds of Israel have failed miserably, so God will come and shepherd them Himself. But God also mentions another shepherd: David. Since King David has been dead for over four hundred years, what does God mean here exactly?

Again, this is a messianic reference. *Read 2 Samuel 7:11–16. For how long would David's descendants rule on the throne?*

God reaffirms His covenant He made with David. At the time of this prophecy, Jerusalem has fallen. There was no king sitting on the throne, so the exiles may have wondered if God had broken His promise He had made to David. Here God reassures His people that He has not forgotten His covenant. He remembers. It will be God's own Son that will sit on the throne, and He will reign forever!

The people's knowledge of the Davidic covenant had actually become a snare for them. They believed they could behave in any way they wanted and Jerusalem would forever remain secure because of God's promise to David. This helps us understand why the people refused to believe the prophecies of both Jeremiah and Ezekiel that Jerusalem would fall. God did not break His promise. Instead, He fulfilled it in an even greater way than David could have ever imagined. God Himself would send His only begotten Son to come and rule as a descendant of David and He would establish a kingdom that would never end! Jesus is the King of kings!

Jesus referenced this promise about Himself in a discussion with the Pharisees.

What question did Jesus ask the Pharisees in Luke 20:41–44?

Here Jesus implies that the promised descendant of David had to be greater than David. How does David affirm this in Psalm 110:1 in speaking of his descendant who would rule after him?

READ EZEKIEL 34:25–29.

When specifically, would the people know that God was the Lord?

Read Matthew 11:28–30. How does Jesus describe His yoke?

God does not remove the yoke of our sin and then send us wandering aimlessly to get lost again or fall off a cliff like a stray sheep! Instead He removes the harsh and oppressive yoke of our accuser and replaces it with His yoke of rest and security.

Peace does not come from being our own shepherd; peace comes from following the guidance of the Good Shepherd.

Truly knowing the Lord leads to greater levels of security and peace. Let's look at just a few words to describe God:

GRACIOUS   SUFFICIENT   WISE   SOVEREIGN   LOVING   POWERFUL

MERCIFUL   KIND   OMNISCIENT   JUST   PERFECT   HOLY   TIMELY

What is an area of your life where you need to know that He is the Lord? For example:

Your finances

Your marriage

A relationship

Your career

Your hopes and dreams

A prodigal family member

An unknown future

Stop, pray, and ask the Lord to reveal Himself to you through this situation. Ask Him to remind you of the attributes of Himself that you are having a hard time trusting in your current circumstance. Commit to seeking Him through prayer and the study of His Word. Ask Him to increase your faith to believe that He is sovereign and wise in all that concerns you today.

We need to be led. Are we more interested in following a person, a church, a beloved Bible study teacher—or our Good Shepherd? Sheep cannot survive without a shepherd, and we are always being led or influenced by something or someone. We were meant to be in a flock and we were meant to listen to the voice of our Good Shepherd.

Conclude today by reading John 10:11–18. Thank your Good Shepherd for laying down His life for you. Ask Him for an ear to know His voice, for Him to speak to you clearly through His Word. Jesus will never run away. No matter how many wolves pursue you, Jesus is your Good Shepherd. He knows you, and He will protect you.

THE DESCENDANT OF DAVID

EZEKIEL 35–36

Does anyone else have children with supersonic hearing? The moment I start talking about food my son can hear me from a million miles away. At the mere mention of a restaurant his ears suddenly perk up. I'm chalking it up to him being a teenage boy who lives in a perpetual state of hunger due to his growing at an incredibly rapid rate, but any discussion about what or where the Wiggenhorns will eat never fails to go unnoticed by him.

The Israelites also dialed into certain topics with amazing clarity. The topic of Messiah. They rested all of their hope on the joyful anticipation of Messiah's arrival. Whenever David is mentioned, their ears tuned in, because the Messiah was also commonly referred to as the Son of David.

Today's reading involves messianic references as well. The return of David. The establishment of David's throne. Both of these perked up the people's ears to mean one thing: this is about the Messiah. Today we dive into more Davidic connections again.

Back in Ezekiel 25, we met Israel's cousins—the Edomites who dwelt on Mount Seir. The Edomites were descendants of Esau, while Israel came from Esau's twin brother, Jacob (God changed Jacob's name to Israel; see Gen. 32:28). These twin brothers held a long-standing rivalry from birth that resulted in perpetual enmity between the two nations they birthed. Even after over four hundred years of no contact, when Moses finally led the people out of Egypt and through the wilderness, the Edomites refused to allow them to pass through their nation (Num. 20:14–21). Though they were technically kin, both grandsons of Abraham, their relations remained unfavorable and they warred against one another for generations.

Do you remember the only one of Israel's kings to ever defeat the marauding Edomites? David. When God starts talking about the Edomites being overthrown, it meant only one thing to Ezekiel's audience: the arrival of the Son of David, the anointed one, the Messiah.

READ EZEKIEL 35:1–5.

Who did the Lord tell Ezekiel to prophesy against?

What does God desire the people of Mount Seir to know?

Interestingly, when the Romans destroyed Jerusalem in AD 70, the Edomites virtually disappeared from history.[33] They become cut off not long after the death and resurrection of the Messiah. God will execute justice on the earth. God said something twice in Ezekiel 35 in regard to the injustices of Edom.

Look at verses 12 and 13. What did God say twice?

Nothing is hidden from the Lord, friend. He sees. He knows. He hears.

Read Ezekiel 36:1–7 and record how many times God grabs their attention with "Hear the Word of the Lord G<small>OD</small>" OR "Thus says the Lord G<small>OD</small>":

God really wants to make sure they are listening, because He is about to tell them something incredible.

Look at Ezekiel 36:8. What wonderful promise did God finally make to His people that they had been waiting to hear for years now?

READ EZEKIEL 36:8–12.

Compare God's plan for Israel to that of Edom from verses 1–5:

EDOM		ISRAEL	
People		People	
Towns		Towns	
Land		Land	
The Result		The Result	

Did you notice something here? God was going to do two completely different things in these nations, but the result would be the same: they would know that He is the Lord. God reveals Himself and the extent of His power and glory through:

1. Judgment of sin

2. Judgment of the oppressor

3. Restoration and blessing of His people

READ EZEKIEL 36:22–23.

What did the Lord have in mind when He chose to restore Israel and remove her impurities from her?

Look at Ezekiel 36:24–32. Finish God's "I will" statements below:

I will

I will

I will

And I will

I will

And I will

And I will

And I will

And I will

And I will

I will

Then you will remember your evil ways, and your deeds that were not good, and you will loathe yourselves for your iniquities and your abominations (Ezek. 36:31).

I have heard countless sermons on all of those things above that God promised to do. I am not sure I have ever heard one sermon on what God tells His people they will do. Our faithful God never fails to keep His promises. But you and I may have forgotten the state of our sinfulness apart from His salvation. It's pretty difficult to revive the one who forgot they were dead and made alive.

But God, being rich in mercy, because of the great love with which
he loved us, even when we were dead in our trespasses, made us alive together
with Christ—by grace you have been saved.

EPHESIANS 2:4–5

A NEW HEART AND A NEW LIFE!

EZEKIEL 37

When I was a young girl, my dad worked in Washington, DC, each spring as a consultant. During spring break, my mom and I got to go visit him. We traveled all over by the Metro rail system taking in our nation's historic sites. One site that struck me most was Arlington National Cemetery. Row upon row of tombstones reminding us of those who gave their lives for our country's preservation and safety stretched out before me. So many I could not see beyond the edges of them or possibly begin to count them all.

Today, we are going to take a trip to Israel's national cemetery, except there are so many bones they have not even been buried. They remain lying in heaps on the valley floor.

READ EZEKIEL 37:1–6.

How did Ezekiel describe the bones?

Finish God's question to Ezekiel and his answer: "Son of Man, can these bones
_____*?*

And I answered, "O Lord GOD*, _____."*

What did God tell Ezekiel to do to the bones (check all that apply):

Prophesy to them

Speak to them

Command them to listen to the Word of the Lord

Tell them they will come to life

Tell the right hands to go find their left ones

What would the bones know as a result?

God gives this vision to Ezekiel the night before the fugitive arrived to announce
Jerusalem's fall.[34] Such news stripped the people of all hope, leaving them dejected
and cut off from God and His promises. The timing of the vision proves as
profound as the promises of which it speaks. Ezekiel's emphasizing the dryness

of the bones means that death occurred a long, long time ago. God's promises to resurrect His people lie outside the realm of possibility apart from the work of God. No wonder Ezekiel answers as he does.

Have you ever had a situation in your life that appeared utterly hopeless and dead to the possibility of change? The plight of humanity on this fallen earth continues to be living through tragic and difficult circumstances in which we cry, "O Lord God, You alone know what good might possibly come from this disaster!"

This prophecy is inextricably tied to the previous chapter when God promises to physically restore Israel as a nation. Ezekiel received both visions simultaneously, and they must be viewed in connection with each other. While Ezekiel 36 discusses the physical resurrection of the nation of Israel, meaning her land would be returned to her and she would become an independent nation again, Ezekiel 37 discusses the spiritual resurrection that will occur in the people of Israel within this new land. This is not a vision about the resurrection of the dead; this is a promise that God will physically restore the land to Israel and spiritually restore the people to a proper relationship with Himself. In light of the news the exiles would receive in the morning that the city of Jerusalem lay in utter ruin before Nebuchadnezzar's mighty army, these promises seemed far-fetched at best and utterly impossible at worst.

Has God ever done the impossible in your life? If so, describe the scenario.

Do you currently have a situation or scenario in your life today that if someone asked you how it might work out, you can only reply, "You alone know, Lord"? *What are some practical steps you can take to believe God has a plan in it and for it?*

When God asks you to believe Him for the impossible, how apt are you to readily obey?

1	5	10
It is hard for me to believe God has His best for me	*I can believe God for some things but struggle with others*	*I am eager for God to challenge me!*

Since we are right in the middle of an exciting scene, let's get back to what happens. *Read Ezekiel 37:7–14. What did Ezekiel do next?*

What was the problem with the reconstructed bones? What were they missing?

Who was Ezekiel to prophesy to next, and what was he to say?

What happened after Ezekiel prophesied?

What would the exiles say in response to the fall of Jerusalem?

How did God respond to the viewpoint regarding their current situation? What did He promise to do for them?

Again, God is not prophesying about the physical resurrection of man. He is talking about spiritual resurrection from death to life. While parts of this prophecy have come to fulfillment with the establishment of Israel as an independent nation, others aspects of the prophecy yet remain to be realized. The nation of Israel still faces tenuous peace and security issues within the world. Many of Jewish descent do not acknowledge Jesus as their Messiah. They remain spiritually dead, but during Christ's millennial reign when He returns, the Jewish people of Israel will finally recognize Jesus as the promised Son of David.

The impossible nature of the prophecy emphasizes that the spiritual awakening of Israel can only be attributable to a work of God. The people could never bring about this awakening themselves. It will necessarily be an act of God. The remedy remains one only He can provide. The nation of Israel depended on the faithfulness of God to bring about their restoration and revival. Likewise, we as modern-day followers of Jesus depend on the work of the Breath, the Spirit of God, to bring about our own spiritual awakening and revival.

We can believe God to:

- Bring us to sanctification

- Increase our faith

- Teach us to pray

- Humble our hearts

- Make us aware of our sin

- Give us wisdom

- Exhibit the fruit of the Spirit in our lives in difficult circumstances and painful relationships

- Experience new levels of victory over sin

I would wager that most of us have a circumstance or a relationship in our lives in which we need the all-powerful, life-giving God to infuse it with His breath. Though we are God's children, we still face situations that seem dead, devoid of hope, or impossible to change. There is no part of our lives that falls outside the sovereignty of God into which He is unable to bring life, hope, or restoration. When we feel hopeless, this passage serves as a great reminder that a drop of hope can always be found, even in the driest of circumstances.

Record Romans 15:13 here:

God cements these promises in Ezekiel 36–37 with one final object lesson.

READ EZEKIEL 37:15–28.

What did God tell Ezekiel to do with the two sticks?

Who did each of the sticks represent?

When God rejoined the nation of Israel, what would be the spiritual result?

Who would rule over them?

Look carefully at verses 24–28 and count how many times God says "forever"
and "forevermore":

I am now humming the "Hallelujah Chorus" from Handel's *Messiah*: "Forever and
ever, forever and ever, hallelujah! Hallelujah!" When God repeats Himself like this,
He really wants us to get it.

The nation of Israel split into two kingdoms, Israel and Judah, after King
Solomon's death in 931 BC. The northern kingdom, Israel, was sometimes called
Ephraim. As one of the original twelve tribes, Ephraim held a large allotment
of land in this northern portion. The southern kingdom contained the city of
Jerusalem and was named after one of Jacob's twelve sons, Judah. God promises
that the people of Israel would again be restored into one single nation rather than
two divided kingdoms.

If we examine these promises closely in these verses, we see that many of them
remain unfilled. Access the news and within five minutes you will see that Israel
does not live in peace. The sanctuary of Yahweh, the temple, remains unbuilt,
and a mosque to worship Allah sits in its place. The fulfillment of these promises
will occur during Christ's return. Most people living in the nation today remain
spiritually dead and separated from Christ. The reference to David points to a
descendant of David who will also be fully divine.[35] Only Jesus, who is both fully
human and fully divine, fits the bill.

When we think of God's great promises of revival of His people in this passage,
a thought continues to rattle in my mind. Could it be that Christians today
continue to spiritually languish in dryness because we have not taken seriously
our call to be watchmen in our generation? We fail to warn our culture of the
dangers ahead and the path to victory through Christ Jesus our Lord, who will

soon come to rule and reign, defeating our enemies once and for all. Do we put our hope in powerful preachers and strategic programs over a move of the Spirit of God? Do we seek human ingenuity for revival or surrender to God's sovereignty, acknowledging that He alone is the breath of life? As long as we continue to try to unlock the door to revival rather than sit in awe before the Lord and say, "O God, You alone know, breathe on Your people," we will wander aimlessly, parched and weary.

As believers in the death and resurrection of Christ Jesus, we have the Holy Spirit within us. Will we live as those who have been spiritually awakened? "They lived and stood on their feet, an exceedingly great army" (Ezek. 37:10). An army stands up to fight. Will we go to battle against our enemy in order to recapture lost souls who have yet to hear of the freedom offered to them in Christ?

ONE LAST BATTLE

EZEKIEL 38–39

When I used to manage my husband's medical practice, we would frequently have medical students come spend a month shadowing him. Jonathan would often assign the student specific articles to read and then they would discuss them the next day. On one occasion, he asked the student a question that included a four-part response, but the student could only remember three of the four steps. The student jokingly brushed it off saying, "Well, three out of four isn't bad!" To which my no-nonsense husband retorted, "Would you want a surgeon cutting your neck open with only 75 percent of the knowledge needed to perform the surgery?" The student got the point and committed to being more prepared in his reading assignments.

About 27 percent of the Scriptures are predictive or prophetic.[36] Sometimes we avoid prophetic writings because the visions are so strange they are hard to understand and it is even harder to comprehend what their fulfillment could possibly look like in our lifetimes or even the distant future. Isaiah's prophecy that the nation of Israel would be born in a day seemed unfathomable even seventy-five years ago, but behold, on May 14, 1948, the modern nation of Israel was birthed (see Isa. 66:8). I think another reason we prefer to avoid prophecy is that it often speaks of punishment or judgment. It speaks of a moment of reckoning for humanity's sinfulness, and we prefer to sweep those sections under the rug and cover them over with pretty promises of grace.

Ezekiel 38–39 falls into that category. These chapters speak of an unthinkable time in Israel's future that we prefer to avoid. We figure we'll worry about these difficulties when we are forced to. But if we pause for a moment, we can take great comfort in a couple of things. First, these events are not outside of the sovereignty of God, so when they occur it does not mean we have been left to chaos or subjugated to evil. Second, God told us these things ahead of time so we would be warned and our faith would not be shaken when they occurred. No one knows when the events of Ezekiel 38–39 will occur. Theologians debate it. Geopolitical analysts speculate about it. Authors' pens muse over it. But God ordained it to occur in His time for His purposes.

READ EZEKIEL 38.

What thoughts would come into the mind of Gog?

How vast do you think Gog's army will be, based on God's description of it?

What events in nature will mark this battle?

What will many nations know when God defeats him in his attack on Israel?

Throughout our study of Ezekiel, the people of Israel have suffered horrific circumstances. We must remember that never once did God tell Ezekiel about difficulty that was to come without explaining His purpose behind it. This is not to say that God *has* to give us His reasons behind all of His activity. Rather, it is an encouraging hope that our God is one of purpose and order, and even when we cannot understand, we can trust that He is working for His greater glory and our greatest good. In "Trust His Heart," Babbie Mason sings of trusting God's character even when we do not understand all that He is doing. All the events in Ezekiel's prophecies fulfilled the purpose of bringing Israel and all the nations of the world into a greater understanding of who God is. Are you allowing God to bring you to a greater understanding of who He is by seeking Him in the events surrounding your own life?

Has God ever allowed you to face great adversity or difficulty in order for His holiness and power to be displayed? Describe what happened:

READ EZEKIEL 39:7–8.

What would God no longer allow, and what will all nations know as a result of this battle?

How does God expound on this idea in Ezekiel 39:21–24?

The nations will be confounded over Israel's incredible victory over this vast army. The world will witness the power and protection of the Lord over His people as He defeats Gog. This battle will most likely occur during the reign of the Antichrist, who will establish a covenant of peace with Israel but will then break it, inciting Gog to pursue this attack. We could cite all manner of scholarly predictions regarding the timing of these events, but there is one thing this prophecy makes epically clear: the nation of Israel will face another monumental battle during her course as a nation in the history of the world. But by the power of God she will be victorious over her enemies and the nations will marvel over it.

But here is the best part. Over fifty times Ezekiel has repeated a variation of the phrase to emphasize God's purpose in carrying forth His plans: Then you/they will know that I am the Lord, but this last time there is the slightest difference with the hugest significance.

Look at Ezekiel 39:28 and finish the verse:

Then they shall know that I am the LORD _____, because I sent them into exile among the nations and then assembled them into their own land.

The God who holds all of human history in His hands, who knows the end from the beginning and who fulfills all things in perfection is our God. He willingly binds Himself *to us*. Do you know that He is yours today? That He chooses to make Himself available to you?

How has He done so? Through the gift of the Holy Spirit. This mighty member of the Trinity remains in our midst working and wooing us toward revival. We will spend our last week together getting to know Him more intimately.

REVIVAL TODAY!

Our Future Hope

WE'VE ONLY JUST BEGUN

LUKE 1

Imagine you had the opportunity to take an all-expenses-paid trip to Europe. You board your flight, arrive in Paris, get off your plane, and take a taxi to the Eiffel Tower. Once there, you stand in awe, relishing the fact that you have finally made it to see this symbol of Paris that you have heard about for years but never laid eyes upon in real life. You grab a croissant and a café au lait and hang out for a couple of hours until the sun sets so you can see this amazing structure lit up at night. Afterward you jump into another taxi and return to the airport, ready to go home. You still have fourteen free nights of lodging throughout Europe to spend however you choose, but instead you say to yourself, "Wow! What an incredible experience. The Eiffel Tower is even more magnificent than I imagined, and now I'm done visiting Europe!"

No Sistine Chapel, Colosseum, Prado, or Louvre. You saw one captivating thing and you're done. Wouldn't that be ridiculous? But some of us have done that in our relationship with God. We come to the marvel of the cross and experience

Jesus' salvation and we say, "Wow! What a great experience I've had with God! I've met Him, He has saved me, and now I'm ready to go home." We forfeit the wonder of all that He is. We pass by the incredible power of the Holy Spirit or the endless depths of the heart of the Father. There is so much more of God we have yet to experience.

Jesus introduced His disciples to the Holy Spirit before He departed and taught them what to expect when He arrived. In Luke's gospel, six people become empowered by the Holy Spirit in the first three chapters alone and the Spirit Himself speaks. The Holy Spirit is mentioned forty-two times in the book of Acts, the counterpart to Luke's gospel. Jesus' arrival ushers in a new work of the Spirit. Jesus' death, resurrection, and departure unleashes new power in the lives of Christ's followers. How familiar are we with this mysterious member of the Trinity? Without the Spirit there cannot be revival. Let's begin by taking a closer look at our first introduction to Him in Luke's gospel.

Let's look carefully at Luke's thoughts regarding the construction of his books.

READ LUKE 1:1–4.

According to Luke, how prolific were the writings about Jesus at the time?

what?

Fill in the blank to describe Luke's work: "It seemed good to me also, having followed all things closely for some time past, to write __orderly__ __account__ *for you, most excellent Theophilus, that you may have certainty concerning the things you have been taught."*

The primary purpose of Luke's gospel is not to teach us about the Holy Spirit, it is to authenticate the claims of Christ: He was indeed the promised Messiah, fully human and fully divine. However, the arrival of the Holy Spirit working with power cannot be separated from the arrival of the Messiah. Therefore, we will see the Spirit at work immediately in Luke's gospel.

READ LUKE 1:5–23.

What would the Holy Spirit do in this passage and through whom?

John the Baptist
Bring people of Israel back to God

In what two ways does Zechariah resemble Ezekiel here?

I'll be honest I didn't
read enough of Ezekiel to know

READ LUKE 1:26–38.

What would the Holy Spirit do in this passage, and what would be the result?

Pregnate Mary

Birth Jesus

Whose throne would Jesus reinstate, and how would this fulfill God's promise to His people in Ezekiel 34:23–24?

Davids

Davids line never ends

READ LUKE 1:39–45.

What did Elizabeth acknowledge about Jesus when she became filled with the Holy Spirit?

He Is Lord

READ LUKE 1:46–49.

Mary would face great shame and humiliation due to her unexplainable pregnancy. But in the presence of the Holy Spirit how does she describe her situation?

Gives Praise

READ LUKE 1:67–80.

How does Zechariah's message under the direction of the Holy Spirit also echo God's promises in Ezekiel 34:1–23?

He will shepherd

Within the very first chapter of Luke's gospel we see the Holy Spirit at work four different times through five different people. Zechariah, Elizabeth, and Mary, and the soon-to-be-born John and Jesus. A new work of the Spirit begins. At the time of John's and Jesus' births, the people of Israel have not heard any word from the Lord for over four hundred years. The last prophet had been Malachi, who offered scathing rebuke of the priesthood of Israel. When the promised messenger arrived of which Malachi prophesied, he would be a refiner and a cleanser of the priesthood. But another would arrive with him, Elijah the prophet. According to Malachi, "He will turn the hearts of fathers to their children and the hearts of children to their fathers," just as Zechariah prophesied regarding his son, John. (See Malachi 4:5–6.) The Holy Spirit also prophesied through Zechariah that John would be filled with the spirit of Elijah, making further connections between Malachi's messenger and this soon-to-be-born miracle baby.

As the Holy Spirit closes His prophecy given through Zechariah, He promises the Messianic revival will bring three things: light, salvation, and peace. Ponder this exercise from my Bible study on the book of Luke, *Unexplainable Jesus: Rediscovering the God You Thought You Knew*: "Some people insist they don't need 'religion' or that all religions are 'the same.' I dare you to find a savior who offers these three things—light, salvation, and peace—unconditionally. And I double dare you to find a person who does not need at least one of these things in their life to a greater degree."[37]

What is an area of your life that feels dark to you right now?

Religion

That feels dead?

Religion

Where there is discord?

Religion

"Jesus came to bring light, salvation, and peace. To you. No matter who you are or what you have done. No matter if you're the one who willingly brought the darkness, death, and discord into your life or if someone else dragged you into it. He came for you. And His light, salvation, and peace that He offers? Well, let's just say, it's unexplainable."[38]

This is the unexplainable revival the world waits for.

UNEXPLAINABLE BEGINNINGS

LUKE 2, 3, 4

Luke continues to alert us to the profound activity of the Holy Spirit in the second chapter of his gospel. Let's dive right in.

READ LUKE 2:22–35.

Who was the Holy Spirit upon, and what had God promised him?

Simeon

He would see the Messiah before death

Fill in the blanks for verse 32: "A light for revelation to the Gentiles *, and for glory to your people* Israel *."*

How might this partially fulfill Ezekiel 36:23, 36 and Ezekiel 37:28?

God has been shown

READ LUKE 2:36–38.

To whom did Anna speak regarding the infant Jesus' arrival in the temple that day?

Joseph and Mary

Anna told her fellow prayer warriors! The Messiah has arrived! He was here in the temple today being dedicated to the Lord!

Next, we see the first step in the unexplainable revival Jesus brings to our lives through the power of the Holy Spirit. Repentance. We have to pause and allow the Holy Spirit to convict us where our hearts have strayed from God.

John the Baptist grew up and then began baptizing people in the Jordan River, symbolizing their repentance from sin and desire to return to the Lord.

READ LUKE 3:10–14.

According to John the Baptist, what does true repentance look like?

Turn from previous ways

What commonality do you see among these three commands?

Stop what stupid thing you were doing previously

How would Jesus baptize us according to Luke 3:16–17?

Holy Spirit and fire

What did the Holy Spirit do when Jesus was baptized in Luke 3:21–22?

Descended in bodily form

How is Jesus described in relation to the Holy Spirit in Luke 4:1? "And Jesus, full of that Holy Spirit *returned from the Jordan and was led by the Spirit in the wilderness."*

How is Jesus described in relation to the Holy Spirit after forty days in the wilderness in Luke 4:14? "And Jesus returned in the power of the Spirit *to Galilee."*

There is a succession of events here that deserve closer examination. First we find an attitude of repentance and a baptism of repentance. The people desire to outwardly proclaim their inward change of heart. They realize true repentance leads to a change in behavior. In all three instances, the call for change by John the Baptist involves their possessions. They must exhibit generosity, integrity, and contentment.

Let's invite the Holy Spirit to spark repentance and revival inside of our own hearts for a moment:

In what ways are you generous? In what areas do you tend to struggle most with selfishness?

Where does your life demonstrate integrity? What areas of your life do you prefer no one knows about because your behavior might not match the image you hope to present to others?

In which areas of your life are you currently content? Where are you discontent?

Based on your answers above, what does the Holy Spirit need to do in your heart to ready you for revival?

I believe this next event in the life of Jesus gives us a glimpse into how revival further occurs: a time of testing. Jesus was led by the Spirit into the wilderness after His baptism for forty days. He was already full of the Holy Spirit as are all believers who have put their faith and trust in Jesus' death and resurrection and invited this glorious salvation into their own lives. Now it is clear that Jesus' ministry comes from the *power* of the Holy Spirit, as His public ministry begins after this testing.

The number forty holds great significance in the Bible. It meant a period of judgment under the prophecy of Ezekiel as he and his fellow exiles would remain in captivity for forty years. It can mean a time of consecration as Moses remained on the mountain with God for forty days and forty nights. It can be a time of preparation as Moses lived forty years in Midian before God returned him to Egypt. It often symbolizes completeness or fullness.

I wonder if many believers forfeit revival and living in the completeness and fullness of the Holy Spirit because we avoid consecrating ourselves or allowing God to take us through a time of preparation. We refuse to cooperate with His refinement process and instead complain over our circumstances or blame others for our misfortunes. We certainly would not be alone in those choices. The Israelites during the time of Ezekiel chose that response. We read that after the time of consecration and testing Jesus was "full of the Holy Spirit" (Luke 4:1), and Luke adds in 4:14 that He returned to Galilee "in the power of the Spirit." If we want the Spirit's power, we need to humble ourselves to God's processes.

What might be some examples of when God put you in a season of consecration or testing?

How does knowing that testing results in a greater demonstration of the Spirit's power change your attitude toward it?

Luke's succession of events for us preceding revival are:

1. Inward repentance

2. Outward response

3. A time of testing or consecration

Sometimes we get the foolish idea that if we have God's favor then we only live in times of blessing. But Ezekiel shows us otherwise. When you feel cast aside, counted out, disregarded and down in the dumps, that's when God does His greatest work. Those are the places where you stand on the edges of true revival. The pathway to power. The gateway to the Holy Spirit doing the unexplainable in your life.

WHAT JESUS TAUGHT ABOUT THE HOLY SPIRIT

LUKE 11:1–13, LUKE 12:10–12, JOHN 16:12–16, ACTS 1:8

Lately on my local Christian radio station I find more songs referencing the Holy Spirit than I can ever remember. There seems to be an awakening to His presence and a deep desire to experience Him in our lives. This excites me! Sometimes however, it seems as though we desire a sensational experience of the Spirit more than conviction by Him. We equate the Spirit's arrival with marvels, wonders, and joy, but not confrontation of the truth. Is it wrong to view Him that way? I think a careful examination of what Jesus taught regarding the Holy Spirit will prove helpful in answering that question.

The first time Jesus specifically mentions the Holy Spirit to His disciples is in Luke 11:1–13. The disciples ask Jesus to teach them how to pray. The disciples were Jewish men. They prayed three times per day, they prayed Sabbath prayers weekly, they had special prayers for certain Jewish holidays and feasts such as Passover and

Shavuot. So these men already knew how to pray. What I think they are really asking is, "Teach us how to pray with the same intimacy toward the Father that you do, Jesus." The disciples had witnessed Jesus praying over weighty decisions, in moments of crisis, and spontaneously in gratitude toward the works of God. They wanted to move beyond the ritualistic prayers of the rabbis, to intimate prayers of relationship. Jesus begins by giving them the Lord's Prayer as a model for prayer, but He goes beyond that. He invites them to understand the heart of the Father to whom they are praying.

Jesus tells them the parable of the friend at midnight (starting at v. 5), insisting that when they approach their Father in prayer, He will certainly answer their request and graciously provide for them what they need. In all Middle Eastern cultures, hospitality is greatly valued. Not to offer a guest something to eat was unthinkable and tantamount to the greatest shame a host could heap upon themselves and their community.[39] Kenneth Bailey explains,

> Furthermore, if a host had an unexpected guest and his neighbor refused to aid him with food in order to provide hospitality, this would be exceedingly shameful, even at midnight when it would be pretty inconvenient to oblige. While many people like to insist the parable is about the neighbor's shamelessness, I think it is actually more about the Father's blamelessness. . . . Jesus is emphasizing that without question the neighbor will answer . . . [and] will even give beyond what is requested.[40]

But Jesus explains to the disciples that their relationship with the Father is even deeper than that of a neighbor—it is the bond of a child to a loving father. What is Jesus' point? Though we as humans are flawed, yet know how to give good things to our children, "how much more will the heavenly Father give the Holy Spirit to those who ask him!" (Luke 11:13). The intimacy with which He prays comes from the Holy Spirit and is equally available to His disciples.

In Luke 11, Jesus speaks of those who desire the Holy Spirit, but in Luke 12, He discusses those who reject the work of the Spirit even when it is right before their eyes. While some may not understand exactly who Jesus is, those who deny the work of the Holy Spirit being displayed through Him will be held accountable for their blasphemy. Jesus insists that the work that He is performing testifies to the power of the Holy Spirit at work in His life and miracles.

What would the Holy Spirit do for the disciples in Luke 12:10–12?

Teach what to say

According to John 16:12–15, what else will the Holy Spirit do for the disciples?

Lead to Truth

What will the Holy Spirit allow the disciples to do according to Acts 1:8?

Power come upon

Let's recap what Jesus said the Holy Spirit would do for His disciples.

1. Help them establish greater intimacy with the Father through prayer

2. Authenticate that Jesus had in fact come from God and that God's power worked through Him by the demonstration of the miracles Christ performed

3. Help the disciples understand what Jesus had taught them while He was with them and to discern truth

4. Enable them to stand strong in moments of trial and punishment by worldly systems

5. Bear witness to Jesus' death and resurrection and share the good news of His offer of eternal life

The Holy Spirit's purpose, according to Jesus, serves to strengthen and embolden the disciples for the work of evangelism and to develop greater intimacy with God. He is not given to provide a sensational worship experience. He does not arrive to put on a requested display of miracles. He is not summoned to change our mental state temporarily as a reprieve from the harshness of the world. Not that any of those things are beyond His ability. He certainly is able to do any of those things as a third member of the triune God. We just do not see Jesus teaching anywhere in Scripture that He is sent to His disciples for that purpose. Yet we hear lots of songs about Him changing the atmosphere, summoned to provide immediate healings, and filling us with awe, relieving our depression and anxiety. The Holy Spirit is meant to authenticate Christ, not authorize a temporary spiritual high. If we want revival, we need to be asking the Holy Spirit to perform the work in us that Jesus taught us to ask Him to do.

Which of the five things numbered above have you asked the Holy Spirit to do in your life? Intimacy miracles discernment Strength opportunity

How might asking Him to do the five things numbered above result in a change in our mental state and perspective on things?

More devotion/desire

Of those five things above, which one do you see as your greatest need from Him today? Why?

The last one

Living in the power of the Holy Spirit marks a life of revival.

THE HOLY SPIRIT IN THE EARLY BELIEVERS

ACTS 2

The Holy Spirit is mentioned forty-two times in the book of Acts. Jesus' promise in Luke 11 that God would give the Holy Spirit to those who asked proved true. The Acts of the Apostles, as this second book of Luke's is sometimes called, could further be explained as "The Acts of the Apostles Operating in the Power of the Holy Spirit." Something dramatic happened on that first Pentecost.

Read Acts 2:1–13 and then take a look at this description from *An Unexplainable Life: Recovering the Wonder and Devotion of the Early Believers*:

> Let's picture the scene. The disciples were gathered together celebrating Pentecost. Most likely Peter is reading from Ezekiel aloud to them: "As I looked, behold, a stormy wind came out of the north . . ." and suddenly Philip shouts out, "Wait, did you guys hear something? Is there a storm kicking up?" Peter dismisses him and continues reading, "and a great cloud, with brightness around it, and

fire flashing forth continually"! James and Andrew chime in, "No! Peter! Look! Flames of fire approaching! Look up! Pay attention!" Thomas begins laughing and shaking his head. "Here we go again! Jesus is going to do something to totally freak me out!" Contemplative John observes the scene and announces, "Others heard that sound too, Philip. Look, they're coming this way!" Peter sits dumbfounded—it's Ezekiel's vision. It's happening before their eyes. Peter quickly scans the rest of the text: "Son of man, I send you to the people of Israel, to nations of rebels, who have rebelled against me," and suddenly Peter is using a Coptic dialect, John is speaking Latin, and Andrew is speaking Greek. What is going on? All the other disciples are speaking in other languages, too. Peter knows they must act. He reads the next section of the text under his breath while trying to take in the scene at the same time. "And you shall speak my words to them, whether they hear or refuse to hear."[41]

God gave the disciples the Holy Spirit so they could speak to the people. At Pentecost, one of the three migratory feasts of the Jewish people, Jews from all over the world, speaking multiple different languages, would converge on Jerusalem.

Revisit Ezekiel 3:1–9. Based on all we have learned of Ezekiel's audience, why had God promised to make Ezekiel's face like flint and his forehead hard when sending His messenger(s) to His people? (This is a euphemism for being resilient and set in purpose.)

READ EZEKIEL 3:17–21.

What tremendous responsibility is being given to the apostles? How does this echo Acts 1:8?

The disciples were about to move into a new mission, one that would be fueled by the Holy Spirit:

> Here it is in living color, brought to mind by the similarity of the wind and the fire—the apostles were the new watchmen of Israel. Though the Israelites quite possibly would not listen to them, the disciples were to warn them and show them the way to repentance through the Lord Jesus Christ. They were not to be afraid, for God promised to give them great resolve in communicating the fact of the resurrection. Now they understood why they were given the Holy Spirit! However, unlike Ezekiel who merely *experienced* the Holy Spirit, they were now *empowered* by the Spirit and therefore able to speak in other languages.[42]

Peter becomes propelled into action and the birth of the early church begins. But this did not just mean a change in behavior for the apostles as the new watchmen; it also meant a change in behavior for all those who heard Peter's message, repented, and put their faith in Jesus Christ as their promised Messiah and payment for sin.

READ ACTS 2:36–43.

Three thousand people coming for baptism in response to Peter's message seems remarkable. And it is. But that act isn't the only truly remarkable thing we should take away: it is that these souls were saved and lives were changed.

READ ACTS 2:42.

What four areas of Christian life were these early believers committed to?

Let's see how we line up in these areas.

First, they devoted themselves to understanding the Word of God and the message of Christ. Check. That's exactly the purpose of this study.

Also important is that they were with other believers as they were taught. This is the meaning of "devoted to the fellowship." Have you worked through this study on your own? Who might you meet up with for your next study?

"The breaking of bread." This is the celebration of the sacrament we call the "Lord's Supper," or Communion. Jesus ate a meal with His disciples the night before His arrest. He explained the meaning of the bread and the cup, and commanded them to "do this in remembrance of me" (see Luke 22:14–21).

Taking part in "the breaking of bread" also means being committed to a local church body. We are meant to remember His sacrifice, be taught in the Word, being involved in fellowship—*with other believers*. And that, my friend, means your local church. This doesn't mean watching the same pastor preach on YouTube every Sunday morning. It means gathering, worshiping, and serving alongside other kingdom members.

Finally, last on the list but certainly not least, the early believers were devoted to prayer.

READ ACTS 2:43.

What happened as a result of the devotion of these believers?

In your own walk with the Lord now, when do you experience "awe coming upon" you?

Perhaps this is a little uncomfortable. Maybe you're been disappointed by a church or by other Christians, but let me encourage you to work through the past as best you can and then move on from that. Let's be brave enough to examine ourselves as we look at our own lives in light of Acts 2:42.

In what ways can you honestly say you're devoted to learning from the Word, being in fellowhip with other believers, taking part in Communion, and prayer? Are other things crowding out your time?

Do you need to sacrifice other things to be more devoted in these areas? Are you willing to take steps?

How, specifically, are you devoted to other Christians?

If you believe your church leadership is not committed to these four areas, are you willing to pray for them? Are you able to appropriately speak to someone in leadership about this?

Do you have a way of becoming aware of needs in your local church body? Do you pray about your part in meeting these needs?

These were challenging to work through, weren't they? But the reward is that by doing so honestly, you have caused Jesus to rejoice by inviting the Holy Spirit to speak to you within your heart. If we have learned anything as we made our way through Ezekiel, it is that the road to revival traces the byways of the heart. Stopping along the way to shine the light of God's grace and truth upon some remote places invites revival. Travel light today, friend. The Holy Spirit, who came with flames of fire, shines equally bright in your own life today.

THE HOLY SPIRIT TODAY

The Holy Spirit is not mentioned much in the Old Testament. He shows up and anoints people for specific tasks, but God's promise through Ezekiel that His Spirit would dwell within them was a dramatically new concept. For what reason was God going to do this? If we look carefully at Ezekiel 36, we see that God has two purposes in mind in putting His Spirit within His people: restoration of relationship with them and to reveal His righteousness.

We see this at Pentecost through Peter's sermon and his invitation for all of Israel to return to the Lord.

What did Peter tell his audience in Acts 2:38–39?

According to Ephesians 1:13–14, when do we receive the Holy Spirit and for what purpose?

Paul echoes these same two purposes in filling us with the Holy Spirit as New Testament believers in his letter to the church at Corinth:

"Or do you not know that your body is a temple of the Holy Spirit within you, whom you have from God? You are not your own, for you were bought with a price. So glorify God in your body" (1 Cor. 6:19–20).

The Holy Spirit residing within us demonstrates restoration between God and us, and as a result, we are to demonstrate God's righteousness by how we conduct ourselves. Paul further explains this conduct by outlining the behaviors of a Spirit-filled life.

Write out Galatians 5:22–23:

The benefits of having the Holy Spirit within us are not merely for our own selves, however. The Holy Spirit gives each person a spiritual gift with which to build up and encourage other believers.

READ 1 CORINTHIANS 12:4–11.

Why are there varieties of gifts according to Paul?

For what purpose are we each given a manifestation of the Spirit?

List some examples of spiritual gifts Paul talks about in this passage:

Who decides what spiritual gift each person is given?

READ 1 CORINTHIANS 12:12–31.

What does Paul say about desiring someone else's spiritual gifts?

READ 1 CORINTHIANS 13:1–13.

With what attitude ought we to exercise our gifts?

READ EPHESIANS 4:11–16.

List at least three outcomes that will occur in the church when believers commit to learning and exercising their spiritual gifts:

What else does the Holy Spirit do for us?

Ezekiel 40–48 outlines the details of a future temple in Jerusalem. When it is constructed, the Spirit of God will once again fill the Holy Place as He did in days of old. If you visit Jerusalem today you can visit the Temple Institute, a museum at which temple artifacts are being collected and refurbished in the belief that they will once again be used when this promised temple becomes reconstructed. These chapters in Ezekiel are eschatological in nature and depict a future time yet to occur in world history. What is interesting though is what the temple and surrounding city of Jerusalem will be called.

What does Ezekiel 48:35 tell us?

We know the Lord is already here in each person's heart who professes the death and resurrection of Jesus Christ for the payment for their sins. The Holy Spirit is within all believers, guaranteeing the full restoration of their relationship with God for all of eternity. We have all of the tools for revival we already need. We don't need a new temple. We don't need another vision. We don't need to return to a previous place or hear a fresh word. We have received the spirit of the living God, the same spirit that raised Christ Jesus from the dead is alive in us. So, what are we waiting for?

Let's revisit one last time some of the attitudes of the people of Israel that prevented them from revival:

1. Unbiblical expectations of how God could or should act

2. Unmet expectations they held of God

3. Dismissal of their sin in comparison to others

4. Blame of their sin on their family members and ancestors, their political rulers, and their religious leaders, but never on themselves

5. A greater desire to see God's justice dispensed than His mercy poured out in the lives of others

6. An unwillingness to accept that there was nothing they could do to save themselves. They preferred works, traditions, and rituals to be the means by which they became revived

Go back and reread that list again. Do you notice any of these attitudes among God's people today? More important, as you reread through that list, pause and ask the Holy Spirit to reveal to you if any of those attitudes remain present in your own life.

Revival starts within. An act of repentance in the heart. Leading to change without. We exhibit the heart of Christ. The fruit of the Spirit. Grace and truth. Zeal and compassion. Resolved purpose and intentional submission. Only a work of the Holy Spirit can do it. And He wants our whole heart before He begins working.

In his classic book on revival, Leonard Ravenhill wrote, "Today God is bypassing men not because they are too ignorant, but because they are too self-sufficient. Brethren, our abilities are our handicaps, and our talents our stumbling blocks!"[43]

God searches for the languishing soul who speaks with full conviction the explanation Christ gave to His disciples: "Apart from me you can do nothing!"

(John 15:5). May we cast aside our assessment of our gifts, our plans to employ them, our knowledge to explain, and our systems to see the Spirit move and instead cast ourselves before a holy God in utter humility and total dependence.

Ravenhill continued, "We have adopted the convenient theory that the Bible is a Book to be explained, whereas first and foremost it is a Book to be believed (and after that to be obeyed)." [44]

Today we choose to believe in You alone: Your power, Your glory, Your plans and purposes for us individually, the church collectively and the world universally. In this moment we lay all upon the altar and pray as Paul exhorted in Romans 12:1–2:

> I appeal to you therefore, brothers, by the mercies of God, to present your bodies as a living sacrifice, holy and acceptable to God, which is your spiritual worship. Do not be conformed to this world, but be transformed by the renewal of your mind, that by testing you may discern what is the will of God, what is good and acceptable and perfect.

This is when the Holy Spirit shall move among us. Who wants revival?

Some parting thoughts:

I first wrote portions of this study over eleven years ago. We had recently moved to Arizona due to my father's failing health, and the difficulties in our lives seemed to snowball. My husband's medical practice that had hired him to set up a satellite office experienced financial issues compelling us to seek alternative employment, but dissolving his employment contract required very expensive legal counsel. I was thrust into full-time employment helping him set up his new practice, along with frequently driving four hours back and forth to my parents' home to provide support for my dad's care. Our children were preschool-age and required lots of time and attention. My husband felt immense pressure to build his practice to provide for our family. It proved to be a very dark time.

To find some sanity and stability during those months I clung to the Bible. I participated in a Bible study that seemed to focus more on me than it did on God and I grew discouraged. I began to cry out to the Lord, *Why does it seem like so many Bible studies focus on how if we just read our Bibles and believe in You, life will be so much better? My life is falling apart. I need a bigger God than this Bible study is offering me. I feel like it's "selling Jesus" rather than really getting to know Him! Does it grieve Your heart, God, that Your people only want Your blessings, but don't really want to know You?* I wasn't sure all of my emotions were entirely true. I was living through a dark season, which oftentimes means you tend to see things rather darkly.

I remember the Lord whispering to me in my heart, "Study the book of Ezekiel and write down what I show you." I had never even read the book of Ezekiel at that point in my life. And I was living through one of the busiest and most exhausting seasons of my life. I shrugged it off, claiming I'd get to the task later. God did not relent. Everywhere I turned I seemed to hear, "Ezekiel." My pastor began quoting from Ezekiel in his sermons. (Tell me, when was the last time your pastor quoted from the book of Ezekiel?) At a stop light, the car in front of me had a license plate that said "Zeke." My son threw a temper tantrum in the grocery cart, and while trying to deal with that I inadvertently ran into a display knocking thirty loaves of Ezekiel bread all over the floor. Someone called into the radio station I was listening to in my minivan, and when the announcer said, "Good morning, brother. What's your name?" I bet you can guess how he responded. "Ezekiel—probably not a name you've heard in a while, am I right?" I laughed inwardly. It seemed I heard that name everywhere I turned.

That afternoon, I opened up my study Bible and began reading the introduction to this strange book. The second sentence in the overview jumped off the page at me. It said in effect, "God's heart was grieved because the people of Israel only wanted His blessings, they didn't want Him." It was exactly the question I had asked God only a few weeks prior. I felt the nudge again. "Study this book and write down everything I show you." So I opened a spiral notebook and began.

Weeks dragged on. My father's health worsened. My mother grew more dependent on my visits. My children grew increasingly restless from the incessant four-hour-long commutes back to California. My husband's separation from his practice got more intense. I continued to read, study, and write. I was not sleeping well and the stress was really taking a toll. One morning after dropping my children off at preschool, I hopped into my minivan to drive home with every intention of taking a two-hour nap. My cellphone rang. It was Nathan's Sunday school teacher. "Oh great," I thought, "now what has he done! I cannot deal with any more problems! I guess I had better just take the call and get it over with!"

Kim sounded a little nervous on the phone. "Hi Erica, I know you don't really know me and I feel a little awkward asking you this. But for the last three weeks every time I sit down to have my quiet time with the Lord and I start praying, the Lord keeps bringing you to mind. I don't want to pry, but are you okay? Is there something I can be praying about for you?"

The floodgates opened. All the pent-up stress erupted. I had to pull over as I sobbed uncontrollably, relaying to her all of the difficulty our family was facing. I concluded, "On top of all of that, God has been having me study the book of Ezekiel and it's kicking my butt with conviction!"

She paused before responding to my highly emotional outburst. "Wow. I'm so sorry. I am wondering something. I am supposed to head up to the mountains tomorrow for a writer's retreat. It's very small, there are only a dozen of us, but one of the women threw her back out this morning and cannot go, so there is an empty spot. I think you are supposed to be there."

I went on that retreat. I learned how to write Bible studies. And I finished writing Ezekiel. But it was simply a study on the prophecies of Ezekiel. It took ten years before I realized God was inviting me into revival through these pages of His

Word. And I needed to experience revival before I could teach revival.

Our God is so patient. His timing is always perfect. He woos and beckons, reveals and restores, day by day, season by season, and circumstance by circumstance. If you have made your way through this study, I believe God has invited you to experience revival. So when people look at your life they say, "Jehovah Shammah." The LORD is there. In your heart. In your countenance. In your perspective and in your life. The work of the Spirit is undeniable.

Pray for it to be so because that is a prayer our God longs to answer for you.

A life marked by hope, peace, joy, and love. A life that shows the world that God is real and He changes people. It's a dark world out there. Go shine bright. Let Romans 15:13 be your light:

> May the God of hope fill you with all joy and peace in believing,
> so that by the power of the Holy Spirit you may abound in hope.

AN UNEXPECTED REVIVAL

ACKNOWLEDGMENTS

To our Wonderful Counselor who left us not alone, but with His powerful Holy Spirit, the only One through whom revival warrants possibility. You are forever the One I want most to please.

To the team at Moody Publishers for entrusting me with the incredible privilege of putting this work into print. Judy Dunagan, a revivalist and ardent prayer warrior in your own right, and Pam Pugh, a deep well of wisdom who waters all words with sweetness and grace—oh, how I thank God for you both! To Ashley Torres who prayerfully and thoughtfully launches every Moody study with excellence— you are brilliant!

To my family who spends several months staring at my computer screen reflecting back onto my face as I study, write, and rewrite again. You get me and I love you for it. You are my world.

To my prayer partner who faithfully links arms and bends knees on Thursdays— for revival. You are one in a million, friend!

To Adam Dalton who pushed me past my Imposter Syndrome. I am grateful for your friendship and partnership in the ministry of words and also your endless supply of sarcasm.

To Kim Erickson who models a life of listening to the Spirit. I love you friend! To Kathe Wunnenberg, from whom we both learned such a life—you get me and you are for me! You are a gift to my life!

To my Quaranteam—where I can always go to "taco 'bout it" when life gets crazy. Thank you for keeping me grounded.

To the Bravo Team—always a text away. One simply cannot be blessed with better friends.

To Jason Lehman—this book would not be here without you taking me to the woodshed and giving me a "Come to Jesus" moment—thank you.

To my agent, Steve Laube, who always tells me I can write even and especially when I feel like I can't.

To the Big C Church—may we again see waves of grace roll fiercely through our halls. May a gust of zeal for lost souls to become anchored to the shores of redemption rip through our hearts. May we experience revival.

NOTES

1. Matthew Henry, *Matthew Henry's Commentary in One Volume* (Grand Rapids: Zondervan, 1961), 1034.

2. The New International Version®, NIV®. Copyright © 1973, 1978, 1984, 2011 by Biblica, Inc.™ Used by permission of Zondervan. All rights reserve worldwide. www.zondervan.com. The "NIV" and "New International Version" are trademarks registered in the United States Patent and Trademark Office by Biblica, Inc.™

3. "Ezekiel did not remain in this position 24 hours a day. . . . He probably remained in this position for a portion of each day as a sign of the sin of Israel and Judah." Charles H. Dyer with Eva Rydelnik in "Ezekiel," *The Moody Bible Commentary,* Michael Rydelnik and Michael Vanlaningham, gen. eds. (Chicago: Moody, 2014), 1213.

4. James Swanson, *Dictionary of Biblical Languages with Semantic Domains: Hebrew (Old Testament)* (Oak Harbor, WA: Logos Research Systems, Inc., 1977). Also see https://www.hebrew4christians.com/Meditations/Musar/musar.html.

5. David Noel Freedman, ed., *Eerdmans Dictionary of the Bible* (Grand Rapids: Eerdmans, 2000). Also see Walter A. Elwell and Barry J. Beitzel, "Knowledge" in *Baker Encyclopedia of the Bible* (Grand Rapids: Baker Book House, 1988).

6. Gerard Van Groningen, "God, Names Of." *Baker Encyclopedia of the Bible* (Grand Rapids: Baker Book House, 1988).

7. Charles Lee Feinberg, *The Prophecy of Ezekiel: The Glory of the Lord* (Eugene, OR: Wipf and Stock Publishers, 2003), 55.

8. *Pinocchio,* directed by Ben Sharpsteen and Hamilton Luske (Walt Disney Productions, 1940).

9. David Platt, *Radical: Taking Back Your Faith from the American Dream* (Colorado Springs: Multnomah Books, 2010), 73.

10. Andrew Murray, *40 Days of Surrender: The Joy of Letting God Lead*, ed. Chad Hood (Raleigh, NC: Better Together Publishing, 2016), 72.

11. J. D. Douglas and Merrill C. Tenney, *New International Bible Dictionary* (Grand Rapids: Zondervan, 1987), 824.

12. Spiros Zohdiates, trans., *The Hebrew Greek Key Word Study Bible* (Grand Rapids: Baker Book House, 1984), 1577.

13. James Swanson, *Dictionary of Biblical Languages with Semantic Domains: Hebrew (Old Testament)* (Oak Harbor, WA: Logos Research Systems, Inc., 1997).

14. Ibid.

15. Ibid.

16. *Merriam-Webster*, s.v. "sodomy," https://www.merriam-webster.com/dictionary/sodomy.

17. John F. Walvoord and Roy B. Zuck, *The Bible Knowledge Commentary Old Testament* (Colorado Springs: David C Cook Publishing, 1983), 1262.

18. Douglas and Tenney, *New International Bible Dictionary*, 286.

19. Merriam-Webster, s.v. "gap," https://www.merriam-webster.com/dictionary/gap.

20. Walvoord and Zuck, *The Bible Knowledge Commentary Old Testament*, 1274.

21. Feinberg, *The Prophecy of Ezekiel*, 138.

22. Ibid., 139.

23. Douglas and Tenney, *New International Bible Dictionary*, 1041.

24. Feinberg, *The Prophecy of Ezekiel*, 48.

25. Douglas and Tenney, *New International Bible Dictionary*, 788.

26. Walvoord and Zuck, *The Bible Knowledge Commentary Old Testament*, 1279.

27. Feinberg, *The Prophecy of Ezekiel*, 152.

28. Douglas and Tenney, *New International Bible Dictionary*, 991.

29. Feinberg, *The Prophecy of Ezekiel*, 161.

30. Walvoord and Zuck, *The Bible Knowledge Commentary Old Testament*, 1283.

31. Ibid., 1289.

32. Oswald Chambers, *My Utmost for His Highest Updated Edition* (Grand Rapids: Discovery House Publishers, 1992), January 2.

33. Douglas and Tenney, *New International Bible Dictionary*, 293.

34. In the form of a clay tablet, the Babylonian Chronicle for the years 605–594 BCE records events from the twenty-first and final year of the Babylonian king Nabopolassar's reign and the first twelve years of King Nebuchadnezzar's reign. The text describes King Nebuchadnezzar's invasion of Jerusalem, including his capture and exile of King Jehoiachin. http://jerusalem.nottingham.ac.uk/items/show/45.

35. Michael Rydelnik and Michael Vanlaningham, gen. eds., *The Moody Bible Commentary* (Chicago: Moody, 2014), 1259.

36. J. B. Payne, *The Encyclopedia of Biblical Prophecy* (Grand Rapids: Baker, 1980), 675.

37. Erica Wiggenhorn, *Unexplainable Jesus: Rediscovering the God You Thought You Knew* (Chicago: Moody, 2019), 36.

38. Ibid., 37.

39. Kenneth E. Bailey, *Poet & Peasant and Through Peasant Eyes: A Literary-Cultural Approach to the Parables in Luke* (Grand Rapids: Eerdmans, 1983), 123.

40. Ibid.

41. Erica Wiggenhorn, *An Unexplainable Life: Recovering the Awe and Wonder of the Early Church* (Chicago: Moody, 2016), 51–52.

42. Ibid., 52–53.

43. Leonard Ravenhill, *Why Revival Tarries* (Grand Rapids: Bethany House Publishers, 1959), 39.

44. Ibid, 71.

MORE FROM ERICA WIGGENHORN

An Unexplainable Life is a call to reignite the mission and movement of the early church individually and collectively. This in-depth, 10-week Bible study challenges our modern-day assumptions, inspires us to reclaim the zeal of the apostles, and invites us to join Jesus in His work today.

978-0-8024-1473-1

The Unexplainable Church is a 10-week inductive study of Acts 13–28 that features scholarly insights, personal reflections, and prompts for application. It will teach by example how to study the Bible deeply, and it will challenge you toward critical life-change: submitting your will to the mission of the church, where life finds its fullest meaning.

978-0-8024-1742-8

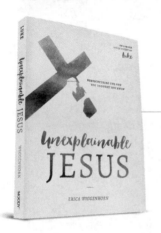

Step into the streets of Jerusalem and encounter the Jewish rabbi who turned the world upside down. After rediscovering Jesus in the pages of the book of Luke—or maybe discovering Him for the very first time—you'll see there is no other plan, goal, ambition, or Person worth following but Jesus.

978-0-8024-1909-5

also available as eBooks

MOODY PUBLISHERS
WOMEN
BIBLE STUDIES

Everyone thinks you've got it together.
But inside, you're asking, "Am I enough?"

No matter how good we look externally, self-doubt is
hard to shake. Erica Wiggenhorn draws from the story of
Moses—the greatest self-doubter in the Bible—to show how
self-doubt is tied closely to self-reliance. Only by casting
yourself on God do you find the true source of strength.

978-0-8024-2331-3 | also available as eBook and audiobook

MOODY
Publishers®

From the Word to Life®

Bible Studies for Women

REFRESHINGLY DEEP BIBLE STUDIES TO DWELL & DELIGHT IN GOD'S WORD

7 FEASTS
978-0-8024-1955-2

AN UNEXPLAINABLE LIFE
978-0-8024-1473-1

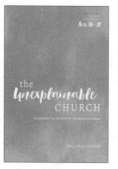

THE UNEXPLAINABLE CHURCH
978-0-8024-1742-8

UNEXPLAINABLE JESUS
978-0-8024-1909-5

WHO DO YOU SAY THAT I AM?
978-0-8024-1550-9

HE IS ENOUGH
978-0-8024-1686-5

KEEPING THE FAITH
978-0-8024-1931-6

ON BENDED KNEE
978-0-8024-1919-4

Explore our Bible studies at
moodypublisherswomen.com

Also available as eBooks

MOODY PUBLISHERS
WOMEN
BIBLE STUDIES

Bible Studies for Women

REFRESHINGLY DEEP BIBLE STUDIES TO
DWELL & DELIGHT IN GOD'S WORD

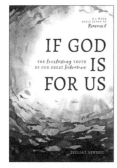

IF GOD IS FOR US
978-0-8024-1713-8

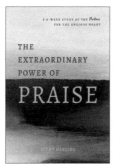

THE EXTRAORDINARY
POWER OF PRAISE
978-0-8024-2009-1

HIS LAST WORDS
978-0-8024-1467-0

I AM FOUND
978-0-8024-1468-7

INCLUDED IN CHRIST
978-0-8024-1591-2

THE WAY HOME
978-0-8024-1983-5

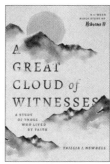

A GREAT CLOUD OF
WITNESSES
978-0-8024-2107-4

HABAKKUK
978-0-8024-1980-4

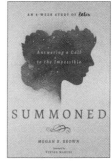

SUMMONED
978-0-8024-2169-2

Explore our Bible studies at
moodypublisherswomen.com

Also available as eBooks

MOODY PUBLISHERS
WOMEN
BIBLE STUDIES